EARTH PONDS

EARTH PONDS

The Country Pond Maker's Guide

TIM MATSON

COUNTRYMAN PRESS · WOODSTOCK, VERMONT

Thanks To All Who Helped

Pond makers & Pond keepers Leonard Cook, Sonny Stearns, Sherm Stebbins, George Williams, Gordon Wilder, Harold and Calvin Day, Jim Malone, Steve Wetmore, Ralph Stevens, Donny Prescott, Joseph and Flo Morse, Peter Orgain, Woody Ransom, Karl Hammer, Blake and Aletta Traendly, Henry Marckes, Hank McGreevey, Bob Huke, and Ray Uline.

Neighbors Eric and Cheslye Darnell, Gerard Stevens, Alan Moats, and Vi Coffin.

Book People Peter Jennison, Chris Lloyd, and the staff of The Countryman Press; Katinka Matson and John Brockman; Guy Russell; Bob Gere, Jeffrey Nintzel, and the Sun Photographic Lab & Gallery.

Parts of *Earth Ponds* appeared in Harrowsmith, Farmstead, and CoEvolution Quarterly.

Book design by Guy Russell
Cover design by Matt Ralph
Digger Pond illustrations by Diane St. Jean
Typeset by Williams Graphic Service
Printed by Halliday Litho

Ian Grainge diagram reprinted with the permission of Harrowsmith Magazine. Copyright 1979 by Camden House Publishing, Ltd.

Fifth Printing
Updated Bibliography and List of Resources

Library of Congress Cataloging in Publication Data

Matson, Tim, 1943–
     Earth ponds.

     1. Water-supply, Rural.   2. Reservoirs.   3. Ponds.
I. Title.
TD927.M434   627'.8   82-2447
                                                             AACR2
ISBN 0-914378-86-4 (pbk.)

Contents

"And like the fishponds of the abbeys and castles of medieval Europe and the Dark Ages, when all the world fell apart in anarchy and disorder, they provide not only food for the table but peace for the soul and an understanding of man's relationship to the universe."

Louis Bromfield
Malabar Farm

For Ellen Langtree

Prologue

How many historians have looked at the evolutionary link between people and ponds? Only Lewis Mumford comes close when he observes that man's manipulation of containers preceeded his tool-making:

> "Our present over-commitment to technics is in part due to a radical misinterpretation of the whole course of human development . . . there is still a tendency to identify tools and machines with technology . . . this practice overlooks the equally vital role of containers: first hearths, pits, traps, cordage; later baskets, bins, byres, houses, to say nothing of still later collective containers like reservoirs . . . ."

I chanced across this thought one night while basking in the glow of the wood stove and a quart of homebrew. A marvelous notion struck me. The "tool" with the most promise for this homestead had to be the pond on the sidehill.

Mumford never sharpens his focus on ponds. Yet pond making first enabled humans to build agricultural settlements with guaranteed irrigation. And through time ponds have done it all: nurtured fish and safeguarded castles, frozen ice for food storage, and turned industrial power. The Chinese built man's most enduring civilization on a foundation of ponds. The revolutionary United States gained independence with the help of ponds that drove mills to produce cider, flour, feed, lumber, and textiles. In fact, life on earth began in a shallow sunlit pond. A single-celled organism with the miraculous ability to reproduce woke up one warm day and has been evolving ever since.

The first deliberate impoundment of water was likely a dammed pond built by beavers big as bears. These creatures changed the planet. Their ponds nursed new plant and animal life, filled subterranean springs, and silted into fertile valley lands. Somebody was watching. In primeval Europe and Scandinavia "lake dwellers" began to build pole houses over water. Climbing ahead of their cave-dwelling kin on the evolutionary ladder, these reformed nomads worked together cutting and trimming trees and floating timbers out of their off-shore building sites. Anchored there amid food and water they lived secure from interlopers. Academics consider the lake dwellers a turning point in human development. They miss seeing that the first lake dwellers were simply aping their neighbors, a colony of beavers.

The Egyptians, who clearly knew the beaver since they depicted its exploits in hieroglyphics, were among the first to practice irrigation; they held water from the spring Nile behind dams for release during drought. About the same time, in beaver-inhabited China, rice growers learned to dam up streams to create fertile paddies. Did beavers inspire those dams and fish ponds? Ask a North American Cherokee. In his cosmology it was a beaver that mated with the Great Spirit, transforming the hostile elements into rich earth.

As late as 1700 a pond civilization of more than 100 million beavers inhabited North America. Streams supported beaver colonies in close succession, as many as 300 to the mile. At Three Forks, Montana, in 1805, Lewis and Clark looked out over beaver ponds stretching to the horizon. Settlers used water from beaver ponds to power the first mills, and clearings around ponds made inviting village sites. Silted ponds became rich meadows for grazing cattle, and beaver dams tempered floods and reserved water during drought.

But beaver hides grew more valued than ponds. Pelts traded with Europeans brought vast sums of money, feeding financial empires like the Astors' and the Hudson Bay Company. *Castoreum*—beaver oil—found an eager market in Europe as a perfume and stimulant. White men and native Americans plundered the wilderness, trapping beaver year round, and by the end of the 19th century the species was close to extinction.

In this century the beaver has been nursed back, but not for its fur or its oil. The beaver is back to build ponds. In New Hampshire, where beaver trapping is carefully regulated, state game superintendent Henry Laramie told the *New Hampshire Times,* "The beaver had probably done more for waterfowl management and other species than anything else in 100 years." In western states beavers are dropped by parachute into national forests to reestablish oases of wildlife in clearcut timberland and to provide buffers against erosion and forest fire. Beaver ponds in Maine are the last refuges of the rare blueback trout. In Mississippi, state wildlife specialists are nurturing a growing duck population by sowing millet in the state's 24,000 acres of beaver ponds.

If beavers lured men into pond making they offered no guarantees. Their technique of damming streams is the most difficult pond making style. In fact, given a suitable pond in a secure neighborhood, a beaver colony will forgo pond making completely and build instead a dwelling lodge with canals for food and timber transport. Where nature has skimped on ponds, beavers dam a body of water deep enough to protect a lodge entrance, prevent freezing of underwater food supplies, and fill transportation canals. If beavers are already established, a simple barrier of saplings and mud is often enough to add a new pond to a stream or headwater. But in virgin terrain it may take the labor of several generations to develop a thriving colony.

After selecting a pond site the beavers begin gnawing down trees, pushing and floating their lumber to the dam. Contrary to myth, beavers do not build dams by felling trees cross-stream. They layer green saplings parallel with the waterflow, freshly-chewed butts upstream about a foot higher than crowns. As the barrier rises, the weight of the dam and the pressure of the current hooks the timbers into the stream bed, like anchors. In a swift stream beavers weigh trees in place with stones and mud. The layered poles knit together and reinforce the bracing. Beavers like young green deciduous saplings best, about five inches at the stump. After some good chewing and a warning thump of the tail, the critter scrambles away, and the tree drops. If the crown tangles and the tree hangs up, the beaver may try again. But the animal is not immune to logging's deadly risks, and he knows it; after a couple of unsuccessful attempts to loosen the snag, the beaver will usually leave the tree hanging.

Where no saplings grow, beavers improvise. "Grass beavers" use cobblestones or chunks of coal gathered from cliffs. Logjam dams are put together from timbers rolled and skidded downhill over snow. After a forest fire, beavers use the charred trees for the dam and reserve undamaged groves for food.

9

As the pond begins to fill, water streaming through the dam plugs the chinks with sediment and brush, and the dam waterproofs itself. If the dam won't hold enough water, the beavers plaster it with mud and grass roots. When the water level reaches an agreeable point, the beavers arrange to maintain it. In some ponds this means keeping a loose dam that seeps water through the structure; in others, a waterfall carries the spill. The most successful beavers build spillways that guide the overflow away from the dam, so not to undermine it.

The pond doesn't always work. A colony may begin a dam near an insufficient timber stand or overestimate the water supply. For a remedy, the beavers might try digging new canals to bring in extra water or timber to heighten the dam. Or they might excavate another foot or two throughout the basin. If the pond still looks too shallow, the colony will scout for a new site and move on.

The lesson of the beaver pond is simple. Natural ponds refuse to seal perfectly, and success is never guaranteed. Beaver ponds evolve non-stop as the animals touch up leaks, channel water, and raise the dam to keep up with incoming sediment. If spring rains and snowmelt blow out the dam, the beavers will build another. Beavers thrive on fixing ponds. Who wouldn't, with webbed hind feet, waterproof fur, and teeth that never quit growing?

* * *

I discovered the art of pond culture by a fluke. A decade ago I was on the lookout for a small farm in Orange County, Vermont, in cahoots with my sweetheart, who had joined me packing for the hills. On one rickety farm we found an old earth pond. I wasn't able to get near it because I was on crutches after a skiing crack-up, and Diana couldn't see much under three feet of snow. But I figured the pond would provide good therapy for my leg,

and she was half-fish at least. So we handed our savings over.

My cast came off after the snowmelt in the spring, and I felt strong enough for swimming. Alas, I found the pond in need of restoration. It had dehydrated; the side-pipe that fed it stream water was clogged. So over the next couple of years I tended the pond and swam my leg back into good shape. I reestablished the smooth flow of stream water, cleared the plugged spillway, hauled silt from the delta where inflow entered the basin, and stocked the pond with rainbow trout. I set up a gravity-feed watering hose from the pond downhill to the barn and garden, and for Christmas I built a redwood sauna close to the shore to enable us to stretch the swimming season full-length between thaw and freeze. That was the beginning of my romance with ponds.

Naturally, according to the law of thermodynamics, something had to give. It turned out to be Diana. We sold the farm, split up the trout, and rambled off to chase our different fates.

Now, seven years down the road, I live in a homemade cabin overlooking a quarter-acre apple-green pond that I sited, cleared and carved in collaboration with a bulldozer sculptor. Happily, not long ago I hooked a mountain mermaid. Together we cultivate most of our own food and collect all our firewood and lumber, with some surplus left over to barter with neighbors in the hills. Seventy-five trout fatten in the pond, and surplus water gravity-feeds a rich market garden and a winter pig. Long-range pond schemes include a fire-fighters' pump, a small hydro generator, a wood-fired sauna, and an ice house. Our holding will swell with pond power.

Beyond this I've found a new dimension in the pleasures of pond making. Of all the bucolic arts and husbandries, pond making alone seems to balance the forces that animate the land—nature and man. You can carve a pond and step back, as people have done since the beginning of history, and the pond comes alive. More than a thousand years ago the Chinese poet Han Yu wrote:

> *Does the bowl*
> *in the garden*
> *mock nature*
> *when night after night*
> *green frogs gather*
> *to prove it's a pool?*
>
> *Who says*
> *you can't make a pond*
> *out of a bowl?*

Pond making was a sacred Eastern tradition. Monks carved ponds beside their temples and shrines to mirror the universe. These shining objects of concentration distilled the Buddha's message. Reflected in the water the moon was pure illusion, empty form. There was nothing to discover but the nature of mind. In the West, pond making was first celebrated in 1559 when Janus Dubravius, Bishop of Bohemia, published *A New Booke of Good Husbandry*. His intention was to reveal "the secret commodities in making fish ponds, and furnishing the same." Yet despite all the practical advantages of earth ponds Dubravius had to confess, "In our country of ponds . . . it may appear that fish with their ponds were instruments more to feed the eyes than for sustenance or food." Thoreau's *Walden* was a later tribute to ponds as objects of contemplation.

If earth ponds stimulate such rich visions—and harvests—can't pond making be seen as an art? (A little Buddhist simplicity wouldn't hurt a bit either.) I didn't appreciate this until I had built my own pond and labored on several others. Then, after watching three ponds empty through faulty spillway piping, and comparing my $850 reservoir with half a dozen $6,000 ponds of similar capacity, I could see why the rate of contemporary pond making was not rising along with the opportunities for low-cost aquaculture.

An aesthetic independence is needed to balance the super-pond mentality of conservation agencies and contractors. Otherwise too many new ponds will wind up in impossible sites with earth embankments sticking up like sore thumbs, pierced with superfluous piping dripping inside and out. Recently, one of our county's best pond builders went broke. "Not enough business," he said. "Who can afford it?" At six thousand bucks, few indeed.

But I have a thriftier vision: a patchwork sea of homemade pond sculptures across the land.

Part I
The Cabin Pond

Digging In

Conceived by a 15-ton Caterpillar one warm June morning, the new pond grew slowly through the summer drought, swelling with the juice of invisible springs. Luck was with me. All around, the Green Mountains were turning brown and the corn stood still. By July, my well, like others nearby, had dried up. From the hill I watched my neighbors drive to the village with jugs for water. When the wind blew, their gardens grew dust. In the early mornings all through the drought I skimmed off clear bucketsful of water for the day's cooking and washing. Then I dove in, stirring up clouds of mud—which bothered me not at all. After my mineral bath I lay in the sunrise to dry while the pond steamed like a giant cappucino. Still later, after irrigating the garden, I brewed coffee for myself. Same water. It was a good year to carve a pond.

Instinct led me to water. Hill life is incomplete without access to a brook or a pond. My shallow spring supplied me well, but my spirit was tinder. I could build a cabin with a chain saw and thrive without electricity, but the cracker-dry sidehill made me chafe. So did the oily outboards in the nearby lake. In early spring I began planning the pond. A likely site lay a stone's throw downhill from the cabin, an acre of alder swamp bubbling with underground springs and fed by an overland vein of mountain water. To be sure, I called on the free counsel of the local conservation agent, who came out and bored into the muck with his auger and pulled out an encouraging amount of watertight clay. He suggested that I dig test holes to gauge soil depth and water supply. In the fall I hired a backhoe cowboy to dig a well, and while he was here I asked him to scoop out two test holes at the site where I envisioned the pond. These pockets filled fast and held water. So when the sun rolled around again in the spring, I started to clear the land.

So far my pond investment had come to about ten dollars in backhoe time and fifty cents in phone calls. Clearing the swamp added little to the list of expenses, but it turned into the toughest effort of the whole endeavor. Armed with a smoking McCulloch 10-10 chain saw, I slogged through a steaming jungle of thick alder, puncturing my boots on glistening stumps and sinking up to my knees in muck. Gradually I discovered a peculiar rhythm in swamp clearing. Plunging deep in mud from tree to tree sapped my strength, but then cutting didn't require much effort; having sunk down to eye level with the base of the tree, I could saw it off at the roots without even bending over. And, despite a full dressing of spring foliage, the alder was light enough to wing over my shoulder into the brush heaps ringed around the site. No dragging heavy timbers through the muck.

A neighbor warned me that bulldozing the debris under is a poor strategy, at best. Rotting organic matter can unplug the best-planned pond.

"She'll leak," he said.

To avoid leaving pockets of brush which would rot, collapse, and lead to the downfall of the pond, I gathered the dead branches and waste wood into piles. These were kept small to dry quickly and burn safely.

And so the pond clearing bloomed in tune with the undulations of backwoods inspiration. In other words, I took my time. In that spirit, I cleared the swamp by Halloween.

A white tide swept into the mountains, and the cabin seemed to float in an ocean of snow. At night by the light of a kerosene lamp I sketched imaginary swimming holes and warmed the journey to spring with dreams of sundrenched swims in my own pond. Slowly the sun came crawling back, with toasty days sandwiched between frost-bitten nights.

Spring traditionally is the season to do anything but build a pond. Bulldozers tend to disappear in the mire. The traction is poor for both excavation and the fine dressing of embankments. Yet late in May the unseasonably dry weather was on my side. I wanted to try it.

I called the agent who had taken the clay tests and asked him to check the site again. He came, eyed the water holes, and guessed it was fit. Of course, it was just a guess. If I wanted "official" Soil Conservation Service collaboration, their office would evaluate contour maps of the watershed above the pond site and blueprint an excavation and piping plan. All for free. But in exchange I would pay construction costs and agree to follow the government's directions explicitly.

"No shortcuts," said the conservation officer.

With an ex-draftee's wariness of Uncle Sam, I put that plan on hold and went out looking for a man with a bulldozer and good grades in pond construction.

Down in the valley lived a friend who had recently put in an elegant pond. Swimming there a year before I had marvelled at the clear water, bright green banks, and gangs of rubbery tadpoles all flourishing in a pond less than a year old. I telephoned him and got the name of his pond builder.

"Hey, by the way," he blurted. "The pond dried up. It's gone."

Built in the fall, his pond filled, froze, and topped off perfectly the next spring. Then, in July, it started to leak. In a few weeks its water level was down six feet. Desperate, my friend poured in a batch of chemical sealant ominously called SS-13. This served only to pollute what remained: a crater-sized mud puddle not even suitable for ducks.

"Dragon vomit," my pal called it.

"Did you talk to the Soil Conservation Service?"

"Nope."

"Test holes?"

"Nope."

I hung up with a sinking feeling. Building ponds was for gamblers. My friend had picked up a bad hand—not enough clay in the subsoil, not enough water, not enough savvy. I had heard of other losses. But I reckoned that I had one strong card: a steadily-flowing spring. Still, I grew wary. Imagine a defoliated crater in your meadow.

Nervously, I called my friend's pond builder. He arrived one bright May day, and we tramped all over the pond site. He didn't say much, except that he had four ponds in his own backyard. We trucked down into the valley so he could look back up at the mountain watershed. It reminded him of the place where he had built a six-acre giant that blew its dam and washed out the neighbors. I took a deep breath and asked him to estimate the price.

"Three thousand dollars."

He must have seen me wince.

"Or put your pond closer to the cabin. That's what I'd

do. Smaller, for just two thousand.''

It looked to me as if a pond close to my cabin would go dry, or float me away some dark and stormy night.

The pond maker itemized vast amounts of dirt, dams, trucking, and piping. On top of it all, he wanted to rebuild my driveway. It added up to much more money than I had imagined. Whatever became of the old-time farm pond? I wondered, as he drove off in his truck.

A couple of days later I visited my neighbors across the valley, a white-haired old couple who tend a farm and a 1000-bucket maple sugarbush. From my desk I can see their cattle grazing and two immense gardens with a family cemetery in between. In times past they had owned my land. Down to sixty acres now, they contented themselves with a trim homestead, pond included. I told Ralph about my encounter with the pond maker. He laughed and said that he had hired a dozer and driver to dig his pond for only $200.

"That was a few years back, mind you."

He said that he knew the marsh where I planned to dig. He had watched it through scores of seasons.

"Should make a fine pond. Thought of it myself."

He recommended a good neighborhood contractor.

Walking home I felt a spatter of rain and sensed a fine afternoon for torching brush. At the edge of the marsh I found a nest holding the shells of hatched woodcock eggs. Good omen.

The brush piles flared. A fireball burst into the spring shower, scorched a birch tree fifty feet away, and sent crimson rainbows shooting through the air. When the smoke cleared, the pond was ready for excavation.

I phoned the neighborhood contractor, and a few days later he drove up in a Cadillac. While we walked over the blackened earth discussing ponds, his wife sat in the car.

I've seen that before: the spiffy auto with a dutiful spouse inside. It's a sign of the reliable old-time Yankee builder. I trusted him. Besides, no one who's really making a living driving rough-riding machines goes around in a truck.

The contractor wanted to begin straightaway while the dry weather held. He estimated one or two days of primary digging, as long as the D-6 didn't sink in the swamp. Later, once the excavated earth had dried, a smaller dozer would dress the embankments. At $35 an hour, he figured on bringing in the pond for about $900.

The pond would be roughly oval in shape, with excavated earth used to build the embankment on the downhill side. No piping would be needed, we agreed. I wanted to try a natural overground spillway, eliminating the need for expensive pond plumbing to carry away excess water. It would be up to me to line the spillway with rocks to prevent erosion. Later, if the overflow began to cut away at the dam, a concrete trench could be built. He cautioned against using a horizontal pipe set at the high-water level to draw off the overflow.

"Water sneaks under there, winter comes along, and it freezes and lifts up the pipe. Then you're right back where you started."

A bottom pipe allowing complete draining of the pond would be unnecessary in this case, he felt. For an additional $500, I considered it unthrifty, to boot.

A roaring bulldozer woke me the next day. Clanking off its trailer and thundering up the hill, the yellow Caterpillar arrived like an earthquake, pumping shock waves through the ground and adrenaline into my veins. Driving the machine was a member of the contractor's dozer team. He trailed a double track of mutilated earth wherever he moved. After maneuvering the Cat into position on the uphill end of the swamp, he paused.

I greeted him, shouting over the roar of the diesel. His name was Sonny. He jumped down and tested his footing on the site, climbed back into the seat, looked at his watch, and started. Later he told me that when he stepped onto that mushy ground he felt sure the dozer would bury itself.

As it turned out, Sonny dug a beautiful pond, eight feet deep in the middle, with no holdups. At one point we saw that the pond wanted to sidetrack into the woods. My chain saw was sharp and well-behaved, which was fortunate because water was filling in fast and Sonny had hit the point of no return. He didn't hesitate a second, smashing through the swamp, brushing past me as I dropped a slew of balsams and cut logs light enough to throw clear.

The transformation from swamp to pond was astounding. After the initial excavation, the pond filled slowly and the embankment dried. Two weeks later Sonny was back for a day with a smaller dozer to tidy up the shore. Then I raked stones out of the earth and piled them near the spillway trench. I seeded the ground with perennial rye grass, and it grew courageously despite the lack of topsoil. Except for minimal mulching I let the grass fight for itself. Fertilizer shedding into the pond would feed algae blooms, not at all conducive to a trout's health.

At the end of a month the pond was five feet deep and quit filling because of the drought. Then September rains brought in new life. The water began to rise. Later in the month, less than four months after excavation, a northeaster blew the leaves off the trees and filled the pond. I had been waiting to find the precise path the spillway would take before laying in the stones. Now, with the pond gushing over, I stood in the drenching rain and watched the water cut the trench. I let out a cheer. I didn't quit until the last rock tumbled into the spillway.

Flood

The day after the pond filled the recoil hit. The storm that had launched the pond kept up. From the cabin I watched the rain rake the water. Then I ducked into a poncho and sloshed down to the dam. The spring that usually fed the pond was flooding like a May brook. I walked around the dam. Whiskers of rye grass poked up through the embankment. In the dozer tracks grass sprouted underwater. Underfoot the earth gushed like a sponge. I followed the spillway away from the pond, checking the embankment. Turning back I began to climb the dam. That's when the recoil hit: the pond was boiling at the rim. I backpedaled down the dam and climbed again. My heart was slamming. Making my fist a transit I sighted the height of the dam over the water: no better than a foot and sinking. Then the crest—and the valley. It looked sure the pond would breach.

For another day the mountains squalled. A lighthouse keeper would have felt right at home in the cabin. Without a step I had moved into a watchtower. But the dam held. One November night the full moon waxed over the basin mooring it under ice. I had all winter to worry if I had carved a teacup under a waterfall.

"Here you go."

Henry Marckes slid a pair of photographs under the stereoscope, and I looked through the glass. It was blurred gray.

"Bring the pictures together so they match along the middle edge."

I fit the images at the center. Instantly I was plucked a thousand feet into the air. Below a mountain loomed in black and white 3-D.

"This is my land?"

"And some. That's close to a square mile."

Hardwood and evergreen saddled the mountain. Evergreens on the west slope, rock ridge for backbone, and broad-leafs on the east. But no cabin, no clearing, no pond. These photographs had been shot ahead of my time. I let my eyes roam the land.

"I'm living under a volcano."

"That's one steep watershed."

Marckes is a doctor of watersheds. With his stereoscope and a cabinet full of aerial shots, he swoops over the mountains to diagnose pond sites. I had called on him at the Randolph office of the Soil Conservation Service.

"Your site is catching runoff from about 10 acres," he calculated.

It's all one forest from a thousand feet. I didn't recognize the land. Then I spotted the four corners below my road, and Marckes pointed to a tear shape he had penciled around the pond site. It wasn't hard to conjure up a wave of runoff gathering along the ridge, spilling down the mountain through the draw that folds across the slope, and finally pouring into the pond basin.

A hundred years ago the ancestor of his 3-D viewer was called a stereophantascope. It resembled a pair of aviator goggles made of laminated wood and glass with a

prop out front to stage the scenery. I once bought one, along with a shoebox full of pictures. Each view card showed two images of the same scene photographed simultaneously through the twin lenses of a stereo camera. Since each lens caught a slightly different perspective, the viewer experienced 3-D sensations: Salvation Army nurses posed in stiff collars, Belgian horses drawing sawlogs over snow, the town stagecoach hitched to a hotel.

The SCS stereoscope acted like my old hand-held viewer with one mutation: now the camera was flying. So each scene became a relief map, each crease in the terrain tangible. Quite a step up from the topo maps published by the U.S. Geological Survey! On the table I saw the watershed as if I were floating over it in a balloon.

I asked Marckes if the ten-acre runoff was too much for the pond.

"Depends. The forest will soak up lots of water before it floods the basin. But if the land gets saturated . . . ." He shrugged. "That's why it's a good idea to measure the watershed *before* you dig the pond."

Marckes handed me a sky-blue paperback brimming with graphs, diagrams, and pond making techniques. It was called *Ponds For Water Supply and Recreation,* published by the SCS.

"You'll see formulas in here for calculating pond capacity according to the size of the watershed. I'd work it out, but I'm packing."

Marckes told me that his job at the SCS had been cut. After a year of pond work he was about to return to his family's farm in Craftsbury. Government funds had been shifted to clean up pollution, and the SCS was pulling out of pond making. Ironically, water protection had bumped off ponds.

For decades Uncle Sam was sugar daddy for country pond makers. After the dust bowl, the Department of Agriculture prescribed ponds for flooding, erosion, and drought. The Civilian Construction Corps of the New Deal built thousands of ponds across the country, and farmers received funds and technical help to carve their own reservoirs. As recently as 1975, in Vermont, the SCS contributed up to 80 percent of the funds needed for farmers to build ponds. But lately, not only farmers have wanted pond making assistance; there has been a migration of homesteaders and gardeners, and the SCS could not afford to dig ponds for them all. So, the agency tightened up funding.

Marckes showed me the figures for Orange County. In 1977 the SCS assisted on 62 ponds, averaging forty hours of work, worth at least $500 a pond on the private market. In 1978 the figure fell to twelve. Four ponds were constructed with SCS cooperation in 1979 and 1980, five in 1981, and only three are planned for 1982.

I was surprised. In my territory I had counted at least a dozen new ponds each summer.

"People are digging without us," Marckes said. He guessed that because the SCS had established such rigid pond making criteria—drain-piping, for instance, was virtually compulsory—many land owners couldn't afford to build to government specifications. Instead they were designing and digging their own. It sounded like my story.

Marckes fished through a stack of papers and pulled out two fat manila envelopes.

"I've been saving these blueprints and excavation plans from my pond training. You should have them."

Then he added a batch of soil surveys, and we shook hands. "Good luck," he said. "You're on your own."

On Ice

The pond maker's Blue Book opens with a map of the United States covered with bars. The map is a dead ringer for the National Arboretum gardening guide, but instead of planting zones, the country is divided into pond zones. Each bar is a regional boundary marking the watershed required to supply one acre-foot of pond storage. An acre-foot is the equivalent of one surface acre covered with one foot of water, or a half-acre covered with two feet, etc. In each acre-foot are 325,851 gallons.

To figure acre-footage I needed to work out the surface acreage of the pond and multiply by the average depth. According to the bar slicing through my territory, the pond needed 1½ acres of watershed to feed each acre-foot. How close a match had I made?

In some circles acreage is measured by plotting terrain on graph paper, cutting out the inscribed area, and weighing the diagram on a scale. That edge of precision was beyond my kitchen balance. I considered calling the pond a circle with a diameter averaging somewhere between the longest and shortest surface crossing, and working out the formula for its area. Then I remembered that folded up in one of Marckes' envelopes was a table-sized sheet of vellum graph paper. I spread it out on the cabin floor. On one side Marckes had drawn a contour map of a pond site with shoreline and embankment elevations. The reverse side was clean. Scaled at one foot per square, there was more than an acre of paper, plenty of space to model my pond.

Winter is a fitting season for scribing a pond: the surveyor walks on water. I blazed the snow-crusted surface the same way I cut up a pie, marking off two perpendicular center lines, with two more slices to bisect the quarters into eighths. Footprints in the snow recorded the measurements for me as I paced off the distance from midpoint to shore. First I paced off the longest axis, thirty-one yards. Then I returned fifteen and one-half paces to the center to make the right-angle quartering cuts, which ran eleven and fourteen yards from the center to the opposite shores. Finding the shoreline was no trouble. Our neighborhood broom hockey squad had shoveled the pond for a couple of moonlit games, and a lip of snow curled up at the shore like the rim around a pie plate.

From the slope overlooking the pond I sighted two more lines to bisect the quarters. I tracked these additional spokes radiating from the center, ranging from eleven to eighteen paces, and turned home to transfer the dimensions to the graph. I centered the long axis on the middle line of the graph and marked it: 93 feet. I added the three other crossings: 72, 84, and 70 feet. Then I sketched in a rough shoreline connecting the eight points at the edge of the pond, emulating its egg shape in freehand connect-the-dots style. Within the circle were 36 perfect blocks of 100 squares: 3600 square feet. Around the banks were 24 incomplete blocks of differing sizes lapping the shore. I totaled the square inside the pond: 1715 square feet. In sum the pond surface added up to 5315 square feet, about one-eighth acre.

Knowing the surface acreage gave me half the formula

for figuring acre-footage. To complete the set I had to multiply the depth of the pond at the dam by 0.4. Anyone who ever waded in a pond knows, of course, that the depth at the dam is only a few inches; pond basin walls are sloped, unlike a swimming pool's. I skimmed ahead and found a sample formula with the dam depth set at 12 feet. What seemed required was the full depth where the embankment starts to rise. Okay, with my toes in the mud near the bottom, I knew my outstretched hands reached about a foot short of the water surface: eight feet according to my steel tape. So the average depth was 3.2 feet. To finish the calculation I multiplied the average depth by the surface acreage—3.2 × ⅛—and came up with .40 acre-feet, or 131,340 gallons.

But the formula was flawed. The weak link was the assumption that the pond depth averages four-tenths the full depth of the bowl. In fact, no two ponds are the same, and the inside slopes vary from shallow to steep, even within the same basin. The two excavation styles, dammed and dugout, produce bowls of different shape. Dammed ponds dug from within have bowls of moderate slope, usually about three-to-one. Dugouts excavated from shore by dragline have basins as steep as two-to-one. So I rounded off my pond to a clean half acre-foot. The basin walls here are steeper than average, and I wanted to smooth out the math. Then I flipped back to the pond map and traced the bar running through my territory to its key. The watershed covered thirteen times the territory needed to supply a half acre-foot! It was big enough to suckle a dozen more small ponds, or a fat one-and-a-half-acre reservoir that would swallow up the cabin, the pond, and three years of clearing. Impossible! Yet there it was: 1½ acres feeds 1 acre-foot, and I had ten acres running into a half acre-foot pond.

Scanning the map I saw only three other territories with watersheds this rich: the coastal Northwest, the southern Appalachians, and Florida. Elsewhere, especially east of the Mississippi River, pond prospects looked more relaxed: four or five acres of drainage to keep up each acre-foot. Alas, was a Vermont pond maker living in a 10-acre watershed obliged to dig a lake? I pulled up close to the woodstove and searched the Blue Book.

Private land users had built more than 2.2 million ponds in the United States by 1969 and many more will be needed in the future. . . .

The demand for water has increased tremendously in recent years. Land users have become aware of the benefits of providing water for many purposes, such as fish producton, recreation, and wildlife habitats. For years farmers and ranchers have been building ponds for livestock water and irrigation. . . .

Locate the pond where the largest storage volume can be obtained with the least amount of earthfill. Do not locate your pond where the failure of the dam could cause loss of life, injury to persons or livestock, damage to residences or industrial buildings, railroads or highways. Be sure that no buried pipelines or cables cross a proposed pond site. Avoid sites under power lines. . . .

The physical characteristics that directly affect the yield of water are relief, soil infiltration, plant cover, and surface storage. Storm characteristics such as amount, intensity, and duration of rainfall also affect water yield. . . .

Average physical conditions in the area are assumed to be the normal runoff-producing characteristics for a drainage area, such as moderate slopes, normal soil infiltration, fair to good plant cover, and normal surface storage. Some adjustments may be necessary to meet local conditions. . . . Reduce the values by as much as 25 percent for drainage areas having extreme runoff producing characteristics. Increase them by as much as 50 percent or more for low runoff producing characteristics. . . .

Low runoff! The forest here is an evergreen blotter, a climax growth of balsams, hemlock, spruce, pine, and half a dozen hardwoods. The ground cover is loamy glacial till of rapid permeability. To put my mind at ease I simply had to "adjust" the watershed factor—by a factor of 1000 percent. I closed the Blue Book and got up to split a log for the fire.

Knock on wood.

Spring

On and off through my first winter on the pond I had been hiring out as a carpenter to raise cash to patch up the hole punched in my bank account by the excavation bill. For a couple of weeks in March I lived on the outskirts of Stowe in a log house that was suffering a facelift. When flatlanders think of Vermont, many think of Stowe. But when Vermonters think of Stowe, they think of money. I felt rich and eager to get home before I spent it all.

Sparkling corn snow lit the trail to the cabin. The moon was hanging from its zenith; it must have been around midnight. As the steep path lifted, it traversed the dam to the slope above the pond. Around the shore a bead of water framed an iridescent iceberg. The pond was shedding its winter coat. Crouching down on the bank where the ice nudged the shore, I leaned on the edge of the floating sphere. It began to glide. I pushed hard. Shimmering like a prism, the iceberg chased the moon west. I headed for the cabin and dreams of spring.

The pond broke out of its frozen pod, drawing up snowmelt until the spillway lunged out like a taproot and the water turned green. Early mornings on my circuit to the mailbox I watched the dam for hints of flooding and clocked the progress of the vaulting sun. Mulch hay on the steep north bank leeched into the water, igniting a bloom of emerald algae. Ahead of meadow grass and garden seed, this flare of chlorophyll was the first sign of new life on the land, as the pond joined robins, geese, and red-winged blackbirds on the early warning line for spring.

Spring runoff flowed down the spillway so serenely that I had to poke the toe of my boot into the water to be sure it was moving. Yet, a few yards below the crest I saw damage. The channel had eroded as frost worked out of the ground. The flanks of the spillway slumped, and a stretch of riprap lay muscled aside where the stream had taken a shortcut.

With a shovel I flattened out the eroding banks and added another layer of stone. Again overflow climbed the shore, sluiced over the two-yard crest and spilled down the exit slope, but the channel held.

I circled the pond with a shovel over my shoulder, hunting erosion. Water sweated out around the embankment like runoff from a cold glass of beer. It seeped into a pool that fed a pair of streams gullying down the tracks in my dirt road. I etched diagonal water bars in the road to detour runoff and paid Peanut Godfrey thirty-five bucks to dump a truckload of good gravel on the soft spots. Then I focused healing rays on the pond to seal the embankment tight. Hell, gravel is an endangered species, and Peanut wanted forty a load next time—if he could find any.

Scouts

Spring poured in, and the blast-effect on the ground-breaking summer smoothed out. The pond silt settled, and the water glowed green and so transparent that I could count stones eight feet down. Like yeast fallen after zymurgy in a crock of lager, sediment dusted the bottom. Tiny craters appeared where rocks had rolled and anchored down, and underwater furrows mapped the spring flow. I've seen water this clear just once: in the Caribbean bays of Carriacou Island where dories smuggling Heineken's beer seemed to levitate over the green brine.

To preserve pond clarity I raked out decaying autumn leaves from the shallows along the east shore. It wasn't a big chore; the pond was well-set for self-cleaning. The valley here runs with the dominate northwest wind, and open high on the hill, the pond is rarely becalmed. Windblown leaves sail to the east side of the pond, catch in the spillway current, and flush downstream to the south.

Under the weight of the D-6 the dam had been compressed tight, a fine trick for holding water, but murder on topsoil and seed. The dam was soggy, with just a fuzz of vegetation to wick off water. Now it wanted strong breezes to evaporate moisture. In the spring winds that obliged, tree trunks bowed around the shore, and I retreated to the cabin for a sheltered outlook. I cranked up the piano stool for an orchestra seat at the southern windows. The sun rolled over the pond, and the wind kicked up a kaleidoscopic chop. As wind and water mixed I saw good omens for trout. Aerated water guarantees fish a strong diet of dissolved oxygen. The richer the oxygen, the better the potential for stock.

In early May I went out to test the water. In the glow of the mirrored sun I hunkered down naked on the north bank, warming up for the plunge. The pond was drawing to life. Where woodcock had nested a year ago I spotted salamanders twining underwater. My orange cat circled the pond stalking frogs, but they squeaked and splashed away. The yellow birch that I had singed with brush fire leafed out in green, and two blue jays dove in and out of its crown, carrying the makings for a nest. I ran to the edge of the bank and leaped. In the evening I bedded in a dozen fingerlings.

No single formula works for stocking fish, but there must be a million notions. At the top of the list is the precaution against stocking until a year after excavation. Evidently, stocking too soon kills fish. I've heard different explanations for this. Newly dug ponds are likely to be unbalanced on the pH scale. In acid water fish develop respiratory problems and hypersensitivity to bacterial parasites. East of the "lime line" that runs straight north from the southern tip of Texas, most ponds test acid. In Illinois, many new fish ponds become fatally acidic because of metallic ores in the ground. Strip mine pits can be reclaimed as fish ponds, but not until high acid has been buffered by incoming leaves and organic matter, or in some cases, chemicals. Other causes of acid water are inorganic fertilizers and sulphurous fungicides leeching from nearby crop land, and acid rain. Alkaline waters are more forgiving, but in the extreme they can be toxic and sterile. Flowing wells and springs may contain high amounts of sulphate, methane, and gases that elevate the alkaline content. In Florida, new ponds tend to be highly alkaline because of rich phosphorous deposits in the earth. Limestone quarry waters start off hard enough to be completely sterile.

The remedy? Like good garden soil, fertile pond water should balance acid and alkaline elements. To temper acid water, pond keepers add ground limestone or unleached hardwood ashes hauled from the wood stove. Manure and compost tend to balance both hard and soft waters. And time helps: the seasonal inflow of nutrients mellows pond water.

The correct pH depends on the type of fish being cultured. Optimum for trout is between 6 and 7—6.5 is best. Most warmwater fish like their water between 5 and 7, although they are more tolerant of extremes. Catfish, for instance, thrive between 5 and 9, with something between 7 and 8.5 best.

I wasn't worried about the pH. Like the surrounding soil that holds the pond, the pH was a bit acid, about 6. But I was concerned about oxygen levels. In Vermont, veteran pond makers know that freshly-dug ponds will suffocate fish. Organic matter on the bottom, unless scraped clean, burns up oxygen in the water as it decays. Local pond makers traditionally postpone stocking until the second year, giving the water a chance to cure.

Henry Marckes had cautioned me about premature stocking. He suggested one old custom for testing pond oxygen.

"Weigh down one end of a red oak plank," he said, "and drop it to the bottom of the pond. Bring it up after a week, and if the end is discolored, it shows a lack of oxygen."

I was short a red oak plank, and lumber prices were sky-high. But the pond had eleven months' seasoning. I decided to take a chance and send out a scouting party of trout to test the water for themselves. At 40 cents apiece, a couple of dozen trout promised to work as well as the best pond meter on the market, and a lot cheaper.

I went for the fish to the west side of Sharon Mountain, the Sunnybrook Trout Hatchery, Vermont's oldest fish farm. Sunnybrook got started more than fifty years ago when Harold Day planted a small forest of pine seedlings on the slopes around his valley stream. As the trees reached lumber girth he cut and hitched sawlogs to the mill and hauled home the lumber for his hatchery. What he couldn't make with homegrown planks and beams, he poured with forty tons of concrete. The ponds he dug by hand.

My knock at the farmhouse door awakened the 80-year old fish farmer from a forenoon nap on the porch. I told Day about my plan to break in the pond with a small stocking of brookies. He nodded and laced up his boots. On the way to net the fry we crossed through a field of small circular earth ponds marbled with trout. Each pond was roughly 15 feet in diameter and three to four feet deep, with a single narrow pier running to the center of the basin. Fresh stream water splashed in by gravity-feed pipe, cooling and aerating the water, and then flowed out a return line to the stream below. Schools of trout graded to age and size filled the ponds.

"Trout like small round earth ponds the best," Day said. "They're easy to manage and easy to aerate, and you can't over-aerate a pond."

In one pond a gang of three-year old rainbows caught

sight of us and gathered near the bank. Day tossed some trout food, and when it hit the water, the trout exploded. A geyser of water blew up for an instant. Then it was gone. So was the food.

"You see, you have to be careful not to overstock," he said. "Trout can bang together when they're feeding and blind themselves."

A water-level outlet poked up in the middle of each pond. Working both as a drain and a filter, the outlet drew a slow whirlpool of water to the center of the basin, catching leaves and debris on a screen. Day told me that the piers doubled as platforms for hanging woodchuck carcasses to rot and drop maggots to feed the fish. He added that he had been having trouble with poachers. A while ago he caught a heron that had been stalking the ponds, and when he shook it upside down, forty trout dropped out. Water rats and snakes also preyed on his small fry, and lately his trout had difficulty spawning. He blamed the acid rain.

We walked downstream to the raceways where the fry were swimming in long, narrow concrete stalls coursing with stream water. Here, under the cover of a post-and-beam barn frame glazed with translucent plastic, the vulnerable small trout lived safe from predators. Day picked up a fish net and walked the plank over a raceway full of four-inch brookies. He scanned the water. He was watching for fish stuck in a seam or a crack in the concrete.

"Trout can't back up," he explained.

After scooping up a netful of fish, he gently tipped 24 fingerlings into a clear plastic bag ballasted with a few inches of fresh water. Then I followed him into a small pine-panelled shed off the north end of the raceways. He poked a rubber hose into the bag of fish, opened the valve on an oxygen tank, and blew up the sack like a balloon.

Tying off the top with baling twine, he set the bag on the floor. The oxygen would keep the fish alive during the drive home, he said. For long journeys he recommended occasional stops to splash up the oxygen by hand.

"Every twenty miles or so. That's the way we used to keep them alive, shipping in milk cans."

Inside the balloon the trout jumped around and drummed water on the plastic skin. Day scooped up a coffee can full of trout chow from a feed bag.

"Once or twice a day," he said, offering the can. "No more than what they'll clean up. This will get you started."

I told Day that I hoped eventually the trout would grow on food from the pond habitat. "I don't like the taste of trout raised on factory feed."

"I like to feed them," Day replied. "But I don't eat them."

He took $9.60 for the fry, and I stuffed the balloon into the front seat of my VW bug. The trout leaped all the way home.

To ease the fish into their new home I mixed a sap bucket full of cold pond water into the sack. I was ready to pour in the trout when I remembered the spillway. I sharpened up two sticks of white birch and fenced the stream with half-inch wire mesh ripped off my cement sand sifter. Then I anchored down the edge of the screen with stones, and the corral was closed. And with a splash I became a fish farmer.

From the slope over the north bay I watched the trout cautiously exploring, clumped together tight as they had lived in the raceways. In a constellation they made regular orbits of the pond, counter-clockwise. That seemed right. It cast them against the flow of the incoming spring. They were as easy to follow as goldfish in a bowl.

Better than any aquarist, however, I had the advantage of seeing the fish in a natural habitat. Through spring the trout spread out. The school broke up into gangs of three or four fish circling the shallows, foraging the bottom, breaking the surface to snap May flies, mosquitoes, and gnats. Working in the garden, I made it a habit to pick a few worms and bugs to throw to the fish. From the cabin, ripples set off by the feeding trout looked like rain.

One morning I found a fish floating near the spillway. I picked it up but found no sign of parasites or injury. I called Day. He told me not to worry.

"You can expect five percent mortality, that's normal."

*   *   *

Brook trout, in spite of the name, make good mountain pond stock. They thrive in oxygen-rich cold water, gaining weight at between 50 and 65 degrees Fahrenheit. Given a seepage of spring water and a little luck, they will spawn in a pond. Not so for the rainbow female, which needs a stream current to spawn. The distinction arose during the Ice Ages, when the glaciers split them up, isolating the rainbow in warmer waters than the brook and making it more stress-resistant. Rainbows survive temperatures as high as 85 F and put on weight over a greater range of temperatures than other trout. They are so adaptable that Norwegian fish farmers keep up with their southern competitors by shifting the rainbows from freshwater ponds in summer to sea cages in winter, where warmer temperatures keep them growing.

The brook trout is another story. His growth rate is slower than the rainbow's, and he demands colder water with rich oxygen levels. At $70F$ he's stressed, and over $77F$ he's dead. As if to make up for this, the brook can spawn naturally in a pond or lake, as well as in a stream.

Its superiority lies in nestmaking. A female rainbow depends on the stream current to protect her eggs under silt and gravel; the brook trout uses her anal fin to scoop out and cover the nest. And at the end of the line, the brook trout is far tastier than the rainbow.

Looking over the pond I saw a distilled farm: shelter, feed, and fencing all in one. Since trout transform about 85 percent of what they eat into food, against 10 percent converted by cattle, the pond promised to grow protein more efficiently than a field. Moreover, because fish inhabit the earth three-dimensionally, they make thriftier stock than animals that tread shoulder-to-shoulder. And they are cold-blooded and float. If I had it as easy as a trout, I'd be warm year round and feel like I weighed 7 ½ pounds, not 150.

*   *   *

No wonder freshwater aquaculture is on the rise. Fish are sponges that take on the flavor of the surrounding water, and the marine fish farmer never knows where the next poison will wash up. I had carved the pond where the freshness of inflow was assured, with no sewage uphill. But I had one concern. Silt. Sonny and the dozer had stripped the sod from the stream that carried the main spring to the pond, simultaneously steepening the slope. Now the channel had eroded and a small delta of silt and sand was building at the shoreline, the first evidence of eutrophication. To buffer the incoming channel I laid up stones like a staircase in the stream. My source was a necklace of boulders around the birch tree overlooking the pond. I planned the stones to mirror the spillway across the water, reverse image, climbing out of the pond. Both channels would reflect my effort to hold the soil: the stone spillway to keep runoff from dissolving the excavation, the stone steps to keep soil from filling it in.

I waited for a warm May morning to begin rolling boulders down the bank. In the shallow water around the spring inlet I shoveled out a footing for the first stones. Then I went prying through the rock pile, hunting flat boulders. Laying the steps was like putting together a half-ton jigsaw puzzle without a picture of the solution.

All afternoon I rolled stones and dove from the rising steps. I finished, standing on the headstone six feet over the water. Down in the valley waves of clover rolled in the wind. The hills glowed grapefruit-green with leafing poplars, the first of spring. In the small plunge pool at the foot of the stones, several trout turned and fed.

Flow to the Garden

The first summer on the hill I turned over a garden and found that quenching the soil's thirst threatened to drain the spring. So I planted a few radishes and greens and sprinkled lightly to keep up a flow of summer salads. When the pond filled it looked like an invitation to beef up the crops. The catch was getting water from the pond to the garden, a steep uphill trek. Just an inch of water over the eight-hundred square foot patch meant 450 gallons. I flirted with the notion of a wind-powered water pump at the edge of the garden until I read the price tag—some scarecrow. I could dig another pond with the money required to raise a windpump. It seemed that it might make more sense to dig another garden.

With two weeks until Memorial Day I had to move fast. Just one site below the pond was low enough to catch both gravity flow and sun. It was a long narrow stretch tangled up in blackberry brambles, open to the west, and sheltered by a steep bank to the east. It fielded plenty of light, which encouraged me, and strong winds, which didn't.

A neighbor was opening a logging road through his woodlot, and the pounding of the bulldozer drew me over. At the controls of the machine sat a large fellow with ear protectors over a baseball cap and a pony tail dangling down his back. His name was Brad, and he looked pleased at the prospect of a little work just around the corner. It didn't take long to stage the garden. Brad skinned the topsoil and heaped it aside. Whittling with his four-way blade he began to pare out the biggest boulders. I told him to use the stones to raise the west side of the garden. Tilting the bed east would deflect the wind and tip runoff back into the soil, instead of downhill. As he worked I followed, picking rocks. After a couple of hours the topsoil was back, and Brad rumbled down the road with thirty bucks in his pocket.

I bought a twenty-dollar dump truckload of rotted cow manure from Ken Doyle's dairy farm. A scheme came to me in the midst of spreading it, so I left the south half of the garden bare. As long as I was going to irrigate greens, why not water some meat? A pig in a portable pen would fertilize and till one end, and next spring I could reverse plots and forget about calling Ken Doyle. That afternoon I caught Gerard Stevens aboard his tractor. He owed me a little for an old wood stove I had traded him, and he plowed and harrowed the garden to scratch his debt. As the sun poured its evening fire over the freshly-dressed ground, I slipped off my boots and paced the earth barefoot. A frog croaked. Down from the pond a wave of cool moist air washed over me.

Three thousand years ago the Chinese began connecting gardens and ponds, using bamboo raised in wetlands for piping. I plugged my garden and pond together with a ten-dollar green vinyl hose. That wasn't the only twist in this 20th century pond culture. Working a solo pond with trout ruled out warmwater fish and mixed cropping. Considering the rich stews cooked up by ancient Eastern pond makers, I felt a pang of envy. Early Chinese farmers planted pond dykes with willow trees. Willow roots helped bind together a sandy embankment; branches were fashioned into fish poles, nets, baskets, paper pulp, and charcoal; the bark yielded salicin, the chemical predecessor of aspirin. Other farmers preferred to plant banana trees around ponds, claiming that water spilling off banana leaves stimulated healthy fish crops. As it happens, banana skins and stems are rich in potash, phosphoric acid, nitrogen, and bacteria, adding up to a shower of well-balanced fertilizer.

East of China, natives of the Hawaiian Islands mixed their own rich blend of pond plants and fish. Written descriptions of island ponds had to wait for the arrival of 18th century Western explorers, but historians now suppose that Pacific pond culture dates back at least two thousand years. By the time Captain Cook put Hawaii on the map in 1778, more than 200 shoal ponds—called *lokos*—circled the islands of Hawaii, Maui, Molokai, Oahu, and Kauai. Some lokos exceeded 500 acres, and fish production totaled two million pounds a year. Land with many lokos was called "fat."

Pond making was a communal project initiated by command of a regional king. Communities worked together gathering coral and rock for the dam. A dam might be raised across the mouth of a small bay or between two close points on the shore, forming a semicircular fish corral. Some dams stretched as long as half a mile and took a year to build. Like beaver dams, the barriers were constructed loosely to permit a flow-through of water. Bamboo gates in the dam were opened to the rising tide, allowing fish to swim in, and then closed. Shallow lokos worked best, producing a rich underwater crop of microbenthes, crusty growths of blue-green algae, diatoms, nematodes, and small crustaceans, which thrived within a couple of feet of the water surface. It was

this underwater crop that growers cultivated to fatten their milkfish and mullet. Thus the loko worked as a fish trap and served feed simultaneously.

Hawaiians also built inland embankment ponds. These lay close to the sea, taking in salt water through ditches and fresh water from springs and streams. Fish netted from the sea grew especially fat in these brackish waters. Two huge embankment ponds in Kailau, Oahu, sustained four varieties of fish and a crop of edible algae called *limu*. A more typical inland pond, however, was a small dugout excavated in a marsh by a farmer who wanted to supplement his field crops. After stocking the pond with a few gourds of awa fry—milkfish—the farmer threw in a ceremonial offering of sweet potatoes. This was considered essential for a healthy crop, since it usually prevented infestations of freshwater grubs and dragonfly larvae. Ponds were planted with islands of taro, a heavy-feeding plant that natives enjoyed eating fresh or fermented into poi. Fish also enjoyed feeding on ripe taro stems, growing so fat and tame that they sometimes knocked over wading children.

Imagine a pond full of fish as big as pigs: it's not just Hawaiian history. Hog-size blue catfish swam the inland waters of this country sixty years ago, along with half-ton sturgeons and two-hundred pound paddlefish with snouts like beaver tails. But pollution killed off those giants, and small ponds now used to safeguard water yield small fish. Of course small fish have their advantages: after fattening up a hundred trout you can take your harvest in skillet-size servings.

I had in mind a more orthodox hog, and I built an eight-by-eight pen with balsam culls from the woods, leaving the bark intact for a back scratch. I set a galvanized watering tub in one corner and dropped in the hose with a faucet screwed to the end. Then I ran the hose up the pond embankment to the water. Standing on the dam I looked down at the pen. With its high corner posts and rough sapling rails, it looked like an ocean fish trap waiting for the tide.

Bishop of Ponds

I named the pig The Bishop and slopped his provender with some freshly-bottled stout to make it stick. The baptism happened a couple of weeks after I dropped him into the pen. He was six weeks old by then, a salmon pink shoat reared by a neighborhood breeder. One afternoon before feeding I watched him nose up a crater in the dirt and tip over his water tub to fill it. I sat on the dam while he wallowed in his mud pond. The timing was right. I had just finished plowing through *A New Booke of Good Husbandry,* the 16th century pond keeper's handbook by the Bohemian bishop Janus Dubravius. Discussing fish diet, Dubravius distinguishes between *Supernas* and *Infernas.* From the "upper part" of the pond, Supernas is summer food: flies and gnats and worms. Infernas, winter food, "is the Slyme and Sande, such as Carpes feede on in the bottom of the Ponde . . . as the places wherein they lie are found made hollow, as swine are wont to make hollow their wallowing places." Wallowing right in front of me was the bishop's medieval vision.

"Hey, Bishop!"

The pig looked up. That was it—I fetched the stout.

* * *

After first appearing in Latin in Zurich in 1559, Dubravius' guide was reprinted three times during the next hundred years. The English translation was published in 1599. It made a fine impression on Issak Walton, who recycled portions of the material in *The Compleat Angler.* The particulars of Dubravius' life are few: Born in Bohemia, student of law in Italy, commander in battle against the Turks, Bishop of Olmutz, and buried in 1553. But his spirit comes through in the book. Dubravius concedes that ponds can be used for swimming, bathing, irrigation, cattle-watering and fowl-raising. (Oddly, he never mentions milling.) But qualities of a different nature interest him. "Can there be a greater or more certaine example of the worthynesse of Pondes," he writes, "then that whereby not onely the owners be made rich through their yearly revenues and rentes, but the measurers and overseers be delivered from slaverie and bondage, and restored to liberty and freedom. . . ." For proof, Dubravius tells the story of William of Berenstenie. "He being required to shew his famlie, what maner of Farme he liked best: That quoth he, which hath plentie of Pondes belonging to it." Heeding William's advice, his son Janus became "the richest Ruler and Alderman of Bohemia and Moravia by the revenues of his Pondes."

What made Bohemian ponds so powerful? The German carp. With its Fu Manchu barbels and armor-like scales, this fish is the perfect draftee for a castle moat. In fact, in Japan, where decorative carp are bred for their kaleidoscopic coloring, the intimidating German carp is shunned because of its military bearing. Looks are deceiving, as Dubravius explains:

". . . Nature made him hue amongst other fish, without damage doing, and hurting no kinde of thing that lyeth in the water. Besides this he hath no gaping mouth armed with teeth, cut close and tender: and as often as he gapeth, his mouth is round, and shyning like a ring. He hath onely two teeth in his mouth, and those very blunt. Blunt also is his back-bone, & soft be his finnes: and a light male covereth all his body, by reason of the continuall comunction and joyning together of the scales. Such a thing also is his forked tayle with the which he as quickly swimmeth over al the Ponde, as if he were roed in a boat: and there lyeth of his owne juice, without any cost to his Maister, bringing this commoditie, that where as he is fatted of his owne, he most delicately feedeth his maister with the pleasant and sweet foode of his body, whether it be roasted, baken, sodden, or salted."

Today in fish ponds around the world carp confirm the bishop's blessing—except in the United States, where the fish has been banished like a heretic. Game fishermen can't stand carp muddying up streams in bottom-feeding frenzies. In China, the "King of Fishes" has been the primary fish of pond culture for several thousand years. Chinese carp growers recently outproduced American catfish farmers eight-to-one per acre, feeding just grass clippings. In Israel, desert ponds full of brackish water produce more than 10,000 tons of carp annually, two-thirds of the country's fish crop. Carp for the table is raised in France, Portugal, the Netherlands, West Germany, Austria, Italy, Japan, and Korea. In many of these countries, farmers raise batches of 2-to-3 pound carp with little or no feed.

Why is such a profitable crop banned in all but 19 of the United States? Must keeping carp out of fishing streams preclude production in ponds? I asked Jim Malone, who has been raising hybrid Chinese carp for a quarter century in Lonoke, Arkansas.

"The trouble here may be that you have an eating style already built up, and the carp doesn't fit," he said. "The problem is bone structure. The fish has thousands of bones imbedded in the flesh. The Europeans bake them and flake off the flesh, and Chinese fry up carp with rice. But it's never caught on here."

So Malone ships his carp within the legal territory for natural control of aquatic moss, weeds, and algae. His white amur, silver, and bighead are biological vacuum cleaners. In warm climates a half-pound carp will put on eleven pounds in one year. That's a lot of weeding—and meat.

Today in Eastern Europe—"Our country of Pondes," as Dubravius called it—fish farming continues, and about 70 percent of production involves carp. To achieve maximum production, fish that feed at different water levels are raised together in a polyculture. Stocking usually is about 70 percent common carp and 25 percent grass carp, with a scattering of catfish, silver carp, and pike. In Hungary, carp and ducks are cultured together; after five years the ponds are drained; for two years they are planted with alfalfa, and then for three years with rice; then they are flooded and stocked again and the cycle resumes. Little or no feed is required to raise crops in this self-fertilizing culture. Pond and field rotation is "still in the research stage," according to the Fish Culture Institute in Szarvas. Yet, if you listen to Dubravius, the formula for pond rotation was settled four hundred years ago:

"Pondes must be renewed & refreshed by having no moysture in them, as feeldes are by lying fallow and untylled. This intermission and drying of Pondes, is most commonly used after eight or nine years, that is to say, after foure or five lawfull fishinges: a lawfull fyshing I call every second yeeres fyshing. And this ceassing and drying of the Pondes must no longer continue then one yeere: duering all which yeere, some profit may also come therof for though the Pondes bottomes lye dry without water, yet you may sowe them with Corne, and use the crop therof. And agayne, after one Sommer be past, fyshe them, if your Carpe there put in, be of three yeeres growth. But and if your Pondes be very olde, so that they lacke force to nouryshe, and therefore are unfruitfull, then one yeeres drynesse is not sufficient, but the second and thyrde yeere you must but lightly eare up the earth, thoroughly douge it, and lastly sowe it with such feede as will easely spring up in barren ground. Of this sort is Mullet seede, and Lupines seed, which all sometimes serve for doung, as often as it is plowed together therwith. The second yeere you may sowe it with feede of more strength, and the third year with the strongest seede of all, and use the crop if you wish. And thus you may see how no year is without his profit, until such time as it is apt agayne for fyshing."

Dubravius never mentions the removal of pond sediment in his prescription for pond renewal. Considering the effectiveness of pond rotation, why should he? Basin drawdown exposes the pond to the antiseptic weathering of the sun and wind. Reeds and other unwanted aquatic weeds are choked, and unwanted fish and predacious insects are eliminated. In the basin soil, where oxygen usually is short, exposure to air accelerates the decompo-sition of organic matter. When legumes are planted in the pond bottom, the nitrogen level of the soil is raised. A follow-up crop of grain further enhances pond fertilization because of plant rooting. As Dubravius saw, millet makes an especially good pond rotation crop. Today we know that millet chokes weeds, entices ducks, and provides a grain more nutritious than wheat, oats, barley or rice.

For many of my neighboring pond keepers, as well as aquaculture scientists, rotation is a lost art. I know one local farmer who hired a dragline operator to dredge his old weed-choked pond. Then he gave away the silt. This generous fellow now has a clean pond, a fertilizer debt, and a $1000 dragline bill. The problem is not merely the influence of machinery: most people just dig one pond, and who wants to give it up for a year or longer? Even a short algae-killing drawdown can be chancey with a solo pond. My friend Steve Wetmore tried it, and halfway down he ran into a drought. To save his pond-irrigated garden, he had to let the basin refill, algae and all.

When it comes time to clean up my pond I may just drain it and dig another. Then again, if I set The Bishop and his successors in the right places, there may be a fresh pond waiting when intermission comes around.

Predators and Prey

I wake up from a nightmare of valkyries swooping down out of the sun. It's an orange summer dawn. Crazy laughter echoes over the cabin, gains pitch, and passes by. Then silence. I jump out of bed. In a moment I'm running barefoot towards the pond through the cold dew, waving my arms and cursing. A blue bird launches from a white birch below the spillway. It flaps away low and fast, cackling with a derisive rattle. I watch it skyline down the valley over the brook and disappear. But the bird will be back. The pond has been discovered by a kingfisher.

The face of the pond is untroubled. No fish scraps beneath the tree, no evidence of plunder. But I've heard that a kingfisher can dive into a pond and pluck up a fish in its beak and swallow it whole. If I lost any trout, how would I know? Counting fish is as hopeless as counting stars.

*   *   *

Earlier in the spring, up the road at Miller Pond, I witnessed my first kingfisher attack. A state hatchery truck rumbling through the valley caught my eye, and I followed. When I pulled in at the boat landing, the glossy black truck was backed down to the water's edge. Standing at the back of the truck a state biologist was netting trout fingerlings out of a vat and ladling them into the pond. For someone accustomed to watching seining operations where fishermen haul up fish by the netful and dump them into the truck, it was a strange sight. As the biologist scooped out the last of the trout and the water behind the truck simmered with confused fingerlings, I saw a bright blue flash. A bird boomeranged off the water and streaked toward the trees across the pond. Then I heard a jubilant shriek, and more laughter from the treetops.

The biologist shrugged.

"I just put in four thousand fingerlings," he said. "There should be plenty for everyone."

Still it wasn't his nickel. I was feeling protective about my trout crop and asked how the state hatcheries defend against kingfishers.

"Trout are pretty vulnerable at first," he admitted. "They're growing so fast that they don't have much intelligence. When a kingfisher hits, they ball up in a knot and won't feed. Later on they get to be quite smart. In Salisbury we used to trap kingfishers until they got wise to the traps. My boss is a bird lover so he wouldn't let me shoot at them. But when I showed him that the losses for the summer were five thousand fry, he changed his mind."

Shooting kingfishers is not standard pond keeping procedure. The 1918 Migratory Bird Treaty Act makes it a federal crime to kill kingfishers, herons, and gulls. Nonetheless, exceptions are made.

"At some of our hatcheries where birds are very troublesome, we have permits," he said. "If you have a commercial operation that is threatened, perhaps the U.S. Fish and Wildlife Service will issue a permit. But we suggest you use whatever scare tactic will work."

I had no urge to murder kingfishers. Besides, in a couple of months I hoped to have my trout fry nursed up to five or six inches, big enough to defend themselves and too big to slide down a kingfisher's gullet. Meanwhile, with the state doing such a good job of feeding the birds, I figured that I had a fighting chance to keep kingfishers off the pond.

There are several traditional strategies for fending off flying predators. Some people stock bigger trout, five to seven inch fry. But they cost more and diminish the potential reward of the harvest. That's no solution for anyone planning to hatch fry of his own. Tree perches, especially the dead branches that kingfishers favor, can be culled from around the pond. However, clear-cutting the shelter belt around a pond seems impractical; trees often provide pond bank reinforcement, as well as shade and a place to hang a hammock. Automatic noise-makers powered by gas cartridges can be set to explode or screech at different intervals; but the birds, if not the pond keepers, are said to become used to the racket. Hatchery professionals cover raceways with netting or wire mesh, or enclose them in a building. And ponds are sometimes overrun with parallel strings crossing overhead on poles 20 to 60 inches apart, like horizontal barrage balloon wires.

I find an antidote that appeared in *Small Farmer's Journal* more appealing. Writing about pond defense, John W. Ball mentions an Oregon neighbor with a rifle-powered cure-all. His friend's pond is in full view of his house, about four hundred yards away. With binoculars he can keep an eye out for predators. On the far side of the pond stands an oil barrel with a target painted on the side. One end of the drum is cut out. The barrel hangs upside down on a six foot tree stump, a huge bell riddled with bullet holes. A couple of signs hang nearby: "Private Rifle Range—Unauthorized Persons Trespass At Their Own Risk." Ball writes, "He explained that these signs seemed to remain in place, although trespass signs along the county road disappeared at intervals. But perhaps the letters weren't significant, for the resonance sent herons, mergansers, and kingfishers with wings flapping to more peaceful areas; and on one occasion, some unidentified critters, with flapping beards, abandoned their seine and fled in a van that had been parked where the roadside signs wouldn't stay. They stay better now."

* * *

Fish is not the only crop that needs protection from predators. Young waterfowl are vulnerable to attack by hawks, and pond keepers fend them off with the same devices that repel kingfishers. Alarms and strings won't keep out a dog, however, so fencing is used. Where it is undesirable to fence a pond all around, waterfowl can be confined to a shoreland corral that overlaps a limited stretch of water.

Another dog-defense system was disclosed to me by Sherm Stebbins, a pond maker from Randolph, Vermont. A bird lover in Weston, Connecticut, had hired Sherm to dig a network of lagoons to make a waterfowl refuge. When the landowner began to worry that the birds would be devoured by neighborhood dogs, Sherm gave it some thought and finished the ponds by surrounding them with a ten-foot moat. The dogs stayed out.

Sherm told me that he had been attracted to ponds in a predatory way himself.

"I got to know the people at the bank because they were lending me money for excavating equipment. One day they called me up and asked me to build a pond on some land they'd repossessed. They couldn't sell the place. Well, the pond helped make the sale, and they made three hundred percent profit on the pond alone. After that, whenever they had trouble selling land, they hired me to dig a pond."

That was nine hundred ponds ago, and predators have a way of becoming prey. The last time I talked to Sherm he announced plans to retire from the pond making business. He had just returned from Beltsville, Maryland, where he had failed to convince Soil Conservation Service policy makers to regionalize construction standards for pond makers, instead of slapping uniform soil discharge rates across the whole country.

"Today the bureaucratic regulations make it impossible to keep up," he complained. Cracking a smile, he added, "I never got rich digging ponds. But I dug a lot of ponds. That's my legacy."

40

Blending In

The crest of summer: bean poles and potato plants showered with blossoms and, thanks to an early morning hosing during a June frost, melons and squash flower, too. Celery grows on an island collared by an irrigation trench. Evenings, I open the faucet on the hose and drop it in the trench; mornings I close it. The celery shoots up. A spray of water knocks Colorado beetles right off the potatoes. A couple of days ago I mailed off an order for a Y coupling and fifty feet of drip hose to run through the melon patch. This is polyculture by hose.

Along the outer rim of the dam I'm picking peas off a fence. At the embankment edge runoff drains away from the basin, so no fertilizer leeches into the pond. The embankment wicks up enough moisture from the pond to keep the peas well-irrigated most of the time, but during a parch I water by hand. Peas make a good dam crop. They fix nitrogen in the soil and they come up early. By the time the water gets up to skinny-dipping temperature, the pond is curtained in green. Can you top a fence that hoists itself and makes delicious soup?

The dam is surprising. I withheld nutrients from the crusty topsoil to preserve water clarity, and it started out an eyesore. Soggy in wet weather, dusty in dry—bulldozer hardpan. I kept my focus on the water. Gradually the hay mulch has broken down, and the rye and clover are coming in strong, along with dandelions and black-eyed Susans. On the outside of the bank I planted strawberries, a good perennial crop for an incline of acid soil.

The dam is ripening into a vast raised bed of wildflowers, berries, and sugar snap peas.

* * *

On the other side of town Woody Ransom bulldozes new hayfields for his dairy farm. "My dream is to drive as far and as straight as I can without turning," he tells me. In the process of terracing the fields, Woody dug a mile of drainage canals and several small ponds. His whimsical contribution to aquaculture was a pair of Muscovy ducks launched a while back. Now there's a flock overrunning the farm, to the delight of his children and his cats.

So which comes first, the raised terrace or the pond? The Chinese pond maker might answer: Neither, they're synonymous. Ancient Chinese town builders commenced work with the excavation of a deep moat around the site; then earth dug from the moat was used to build a defensive wall. When Marco Polo returned to Venice from his Asian explorations, among the wonders of China he reported seeing a hill "made by art" from the earth dug out of a lake excavation. The hill sat about a bowshot off from the palace of the Khan of the Mogol Dynasty. Polo wrote, "It is a good hundred paces in height and a mile in compass." To picture the lake, invert the hill and fill with water.

* * *

Out on the dam I'm propping up the sagging pea fence against the weight of six-foot vines. I haven't seen a fish in days. I begin to pace the dam, searching the water. Nothing. I step to the top of the waterfall for a sight line to cut the sun's glare. The view to the bottom opens up. The trout have vanished. Did the kingfisher finish his mission while I was out? I put on my mask and jump. Swimming down to the basin floor I extend my arms. An inch from my fingers a trout darts away. Then another. Sunlight filtering through the water illuminates their spines, dappled in shades of sand and clay. The fish look precisely like the bottom of the pond. They are dressed in camouflage.

A fish tale explains it: Once upon a time a young angler was working the Test, an English trout stream. A dark trout stood out in the clear water. The fisherman began casting. No luck. Again and again he tried, but the fish would not budge. Along came an old man who watched this lackluster contest briefly, then stepped up to the young angler and tapped him on the shoulder. "You'll never have a chance with him," he said. "He's blind."

Brian Curtis recalls that morning on the Test in his book *The Life Story of The Fish*. He learned that day that most trout change color to protect themselves, like chameleons. Naturally, to produce camouflage they need to see. The blind trout stood out like a black olive in a dry martini. The moral? In the ken of the fly fisherman it pays to be a blind trout. Here, in the realm of the kingfisher, I was glad to see the trout blending in.

*   *   *

Perhaps it was fisherman's luck that turned my cabin into a watchtower over the water. Or magic. I had staked the foundation with no thought of a pond. Now I wouldn't have it any other way. Living over water is the greatest delight of inhabiting mountain terrain—a pleasure I share with ancient kings who raised "spirit towers" over their ponds. The notion that divine spirits inhabited ponds was strong through Asia and continues today in Buddhist strongholds. In China, Tibet, and Japan, towers and temples rose over natural and manmade spirit ponds. These ponds were considered to be the dwellings of invisible water dragons, oracles, and protective goddesses, not to mention fantastic schools of very real iridescent goldfish and carp bred in dazzling colors and shapes. A bit of jade tossed into one of these ponds was hoped to bring a Chinese woman good luck in love, which might come in handy if she happened to catch the eye of Emperor Te Tsung; he kept his harem marooned in the Pondweed Palace on an island in a pond north of Changan.

In Tibet, ponds and lakes were consulted for signs of future events and reincarnations. The Dali Lama was chosen in consultation with an oracle lake called Lhamo Latso, home of his goddess protectress Pandam Lhambo. And when the Dali Lama took his place as Buddhist leader, he lived in the Potola Palace in Tibet's capital, Lhasa, overlooking Serpent Lake. According to the elder brother of the currently exiled Dali Lama, it is:

> "a perfect little lake barely three hundred yards long. This is one of the lovliest parts of the city . . . in the middle is Lo Khang, or House of the Serpent. Plants and flowering shrubs seem to grow more richly here than anywhere else, and on a still day the Serpent Lake reflects the image of the Potola towering above it. This is the place the people of Lhasa love to visit during the summer, both to worship in the little island temple and simply enjoy themselves."

Pond spirits were also revered by Chinese poets, who loved their water almost as much as their wine. Many were the unknown poets of the *Shih Ching,* the oldest anthology of Chinese songs and a main text of Confucian education. Here is some of the ballad of "King Wen's Spirit Tower":

> *He measured out his spirit tower*
> *Measured it and planned it;*
> *All the people rushed to work*
> *And they built it in a day . . .*
> *Doe and stag so sleek*
> *And the white birds glisten.*
> *The king stands by his spirit pond*
> *Where fishes leap around.*

Taoist recluse Ch'ang Chien wrote of the solace a pond held for common folk in "Visit To The Broken Hill Temple":

> *At the break of day I come to an old temple,*
> *As the first rays of the sun glow on the treetops.*
> *A path in the bamboo grove leads to a quiet retreat—*
> *A meditation hall hidden behind flowering boughs.*
> *Here, mountain scenery delights the birds,*
> *And the reflections in the pond empty a man's mind.*

Most magical of water bards, perhaps, was Han Yu:

> *In dawn's light I close my books and sit*
> *watching the high ridges of the Southern Mountains*
> *below which, the clear pool's water*
> *where dragons, chilled cold can be caught . . . .*

Often, old poets turned to water at the end. Lying ill in a boat on Lake Tung Ting, Tu Fu wrote his last poem:

> *Floating, floating, what am I like*
> *between earth and sky, a gull alone.*

Indeed, many Chinese were buried with a bowl of water and a pair of fish to guarantee eternity in a spirit tower overlooking their own pond.

And what do my neighbors make of pond spirits? One summer day I took a look, flying over the Green Mountains with a friend who needed to pad his log book. I marked our chart with ponds so that in the twilight we could find our way home down a path of silver blue reservoirs. Sheets of water waved across the horizon, mountains of ponds. I remember two especially. The first was raw, just beginning to fill. In its shallows flashed an image of white birch trees. At the other end a dragline excavator cast and reeled his steel clamshell. We took a slow turn over the pond, admiring the work of an earth sculptor with a purpose. Gravestones in a country cemetery marked the watershed surrounding the other pond. Monuments stood reflected in a liquid mirror, and the grassy banks grew thick and green: mountain spirits blending into their own reflections.

Part II
Pond Sculpture

Siting
Excavation
Spillways
The Pond Keeper's Seasons

Here pond maker Ray Uline begins to carve out a quarter-acre reservoir in Lyme, New Hampshire, with his pet seven-ton Cat. "She's a good ol' gal," says Ray. "Hardly ever gets stuck, long as you mind what you're doing." Working in the spring-fed sidehill hollow, he uses the solo bulldozer to chisel the pond, from site clearing through final landscaping. In classic hill country style he takes up the earth excavated from the basin to make the embankment for this "dug-and-dammed" impoundment.

As Ray shapes the dam on the downhill side of the site, he keeps a drainage ditch open in the center. Thus watershed runoff and spring-flow stream out of the excavation, keeping the muddy basin firm enough to support the bulldozer. No precious time is lost hauling the machine out of the muck.

Scraping bottom in the pond basin Ray searches for flaws in the earth seal—clusters of pervious stone or gravel that would be the source of potential leaks. He carves out these patches and substitutes watertight soil. A good seal is the best defense against seepage. Pond makers who claim they can waterproof impossible sites with chemical additives and underwater dynamite blasts should be run out of town.

Like a potter's bowl, the earth pond is molded with a blend of materials. In addition to drawing a sufficient supply of water, this site consists of good watertight soil: about 10 to 20 percent clay and an even mix of silt, sand, and gravel. Preliminary test holes in the pond basin are crucial in evaluating the worthiness of a site.

47

Holding water after a storm, the pond shows an early sign of success. Later, after it has filled and the silty water has cleared, brook trout will be stocked. They will find shade and shelter under the twin boulders that Ray saddled on the shoreline. With some luck, the trout will spawn their eggs in the gravel bed that he carefully spread over the incoming spring channel. While Ray finishes up the dam, a young neighbor tests the waters.

Like a sculptor driving a roaring six-foot chisel, Ray rides above his giant blade, filling in the drainage ditch and shaping the slope of the earth embankment. "My ponds have lots of character," he says. "I give them a special curve." To prevent the dam from eroding, Ray abides by a cardinal rule of pond making: Bank the dam no steeper than 3:1.

Throughout the foundation of the dam, topsoil, stumps, and roots have been cleared to help the embankment adhere to the ground. As the rim of the pond is raised, the weight of the bulldozer packs the earth, making the enclosure watertight. Here at the north end of the dam, Ray uses his blade like a trowel to seal the butt joint that splices the embankment to the hillside. This seam usually makes the best site for the earth spillway, since the slope provides a natural stronghold against erosion. An overland spillway is preferable to underground plumbing, which can double the cost of a pond this size and leak, to boot.

Cloud in the ground, the newborn pond will work wonders for its owners, who plan to build a house overlooking the water. Cool swimming holes inspire hot summer carpenters and store water for mortar mixing, gardening, and chilling homebrew. For settlers, pond sculpture often precedes ground breaking for a home. A note for gamblers: According to a rough rule of thumb, the value of a finished pond is triple its construction cost.

Siting

Earth ponds take shape in two basic molds: *dammed* or *dugout*. Choosing between the two is the simplest part of the pond making process. The form is implicit in the site. To dam or to dig? The land reveals the answer.

The ideal site for a dammed pond is a wet hollow lying between two steep banks close together. Such sites are found often at the headwaters of small springs, streams, or watercourses that are dry part of the year. An earth dam can be built across the water between the banks using fill trucked to the site. But the pond maker must be careful to avoid building an earth dam across a stream that runs year round, or that drains a large watershed, unless a major engineering project can be supported, with state approval. Besides, with fill and trucking costs rising everyday, a small pond dammed with imported earth costs as much as a big one used to.

Most favored today in rolling terrain is the *dug-and-dammed* pond, built where excavation of the pond basin will yield enough earth for the embankment. The dug-and-dammed pond is the most efficient building style in hill country. Earth is excavated from the site, simultaneously hollowing out the pond basin and providing fill to build the dam.

On flat terrain where the water table is close to the ground, or where a nearby stream or well can be turned in, a dugout pond works best. With a shovel, backhoe, bulldozer, or dragline, the builder carves out a hole in the earth and the pond fills. A small dugout can be excavated in a day or two. The water source may be runoff, ground springs, stream diversion, piped well water, or even roof catch. Where the earth is too porous to hold water, some dugout makers lay in a liner of plastic, concrete, or wood. Steer away from so-called "liquid sealers," which often don't work.

The Site

More than simply choosing a pond site, the pond maker must discover where earth and water can be joined to give birth to a reservoir. You may have a notion of a pond site, perhaps a swampy hollow that catches hillside runoff, or land close by springs or a stream. There's no substitute for native instinct. If your kinship with the land is close, you will sense where the water veins run and not misread a rush of snowmelt for a steady spring.

But to develop that instinct takes time. How does the pond maker who has been on the land only a few seasons substitute an objective system of pond siting for divine intuition?

The surest pond auger is a watershed portrait top to bottom. Every square foot of land that funnels precipitation and ground water to the pond site will affect the potential volume and water quality of the reservoir. Is the water pouring through your terrain rich enough to fill a pond? Will the basin hold water? Lacking these elements no one can bring a pond from the earth.

Watch how rainfall runs from the highest point of your watershed to its lowest boundaries. Does runoff gather suggestively in a marsh? Might a running stream or

spring be channeled to a pond site? Do springs and streams hold up during summer parches? What kind of subterranean foundation runs under your watershed and pond site? Examination of the earth's anatomy is the beginning of good pond making.

On the way to finding a pond site, certain maps and charts offer guides. United States Geological Survey Topographic Maps detail contours and waterways. Topo maps come in two scales, the 15 and 7½ inch series. Preferable is the larger scale, more detailed 7½ inch map, if available. These maps help with acreage calculations essential to estimating watershed runoff and thus a fitting pond size. Often the maps are stocked by bookstores or sporting outfitters. Otherwise write to the U.S. Department of Interior, Geological Survey, Arlington, Virginia 22202. Ask for the USGS Index Map of your state. From this index you can determine which quadrangle covers your terrain.

Aerial photographs in two forms are available at your district Soil Conservation Service office. *Conservation Plan Maps* are aerial shots that cover about one square mile: roads, buildings, lakes, ponds, waterways, and ground cover show up. *Stereoscopic Aerial Photographs* give 3-D visions of your watershed. By tracing a planimeter over the contoured stereo image, your SCS agent can measure the boundaries of land that drain to the pond site, calculate watershed acreage, and recommend pond size.

Soil Survey Interpretations from the SCS office provide another source of watershed information. These interpretations include recommendations on reservoirs and embankments, as well as the potential for wildlife, crops and trees. Without digging a scoop of dirt the pond maker can assemble these maps, photographs, and data to make a first estimate of pond prospects.

The Law

Once a rough determination of location and pond size is made, it's time to check into pond making regulations. Every pond is unique and so is every state. The laws governing pond construction vary considerably. Here in Vermont, no permit was needed for my pond because its capacity fell well below 500,000 cubic feet—roughly one surface acre averaging ten feet deep. Bigger reservoirs require a permit from the Department of Water Resources and the Department of Environmental Conservation. If you don't know the agency covering your terrain, check with the local Soil Conservation Service for quick counsel. The office of the state governor is another good source for information.

Soil Tests

Several times I've stood with a pond maker who neglected soil tests, gazing into a dry crater. It's a sorry sight—and a reminder that in excessively porous soil an earth pond will not hold water. Naturally, all earth ponds seep; the good ones keep it to a minimum.

Ideally soil is tested in late summer or fall, before the rains. Spring testing results in overestimates of runoff and impermeability. Begin probing potential sites with a soil auger. This steel bit gets into the earth to test for rock, ledge, and soil quality. Your Soil Conservation Service agent is available for this chore, but ponds may be low priority on his list. Why wait? Work it out for yourself. Borrow or rent an auger if you don't want to buy one. Make soil borings over each pond site being considered. If you consistently hit rock at a uniform level, it's probably ledge. Ledge or bedrock may lie deep enough to permit excavation of a pond, but fissures in the rock will drain water, especially down vertical grain. Since vigorous springs often surface in ledgey areas, the careful pond maker will site downhill from the spring, not astride it.

A good pond site will permit borings to a depth of four to eight feet. To determine soil quality, unscrew the auger from the earth and examine the material extracted at the tip. Coarse-textured sands and sand-gravel blends are extremely porous and will not hold water. Watertight clay, silty clay, and sandy clay soils make excellent pond materials. Test the soil by compressing a handful into a ball. A good clay or silty clay will hold together in a moist lump of fine-textured earth.

Another method of estimating soil imperviousness is to measure the proportion of sand, silt, and clay in a sample of earth. You will need a large jar with vertical sides; a half-gallon orange juice bottle works well. Filter a soil sample through a half-inch screen, removing pebbles and gravel. Fill the jar ⅓ full with the soil sample, top off with water, and cap. Shake it up and then set aside for 24 hours. The coarse sandy material will settle first, then silt, and finally clay. The best reservoir material consists of particles ranging from small gravel or coarse sand to fine sand and clay. Measure the proportions of sand, silt, and clay. The top stratum of clay should comprise about 20 percent.

Favorable soil samples combined with indications of ledge-free earth cue the next step in pond siting: test pits. You will want to hire a backhoe, unless you plan to dig a number of eight-to-ten foot deep pits by hand. Again, the best season for these tests is the dry spell prior to autumn rains. Dry season excavation minimizes chances of the backhoe wasting time and money by getting mired in the mud or ripping up soggy turf. Shop around for a skillful backhoe operator, preferably with pond making experience. Be sure your site presents no obstructions to the backhoe—no transmission wires over the pond site to snare construction equipment, no electric lines over or underground, and no pipes.

If you must cut a path to give the backhoe access to the site, be sure to clear ground around each test pit so the machine can heap soil on the downstream side of each digging. Otherwise, rain will wash earth back into the pit. A chain saw is handy on a brushy site, especially if the pits are picked on the spot.

Before beginning test pit excavation, stake out the approximate pond shoreline. On level ground, where a dugout pond is filling, it's simple to mark the imaginary shoreline. On sloping terrain, suited to a dug-and-dammed pond, it helps to visualize the shoreline by standing at the lowest edge of the pond area—the location of the dam—so that your eyes are in a plane with the desired water level. Remember that you want a minimum of about five to six feet of water in the pond. At this time, a hand-sighting level or transit aids the process. Inexpensive sighting levels are available at Army-Navy outfits or sport suppliers. In a pinch use a poor man's transit: set up a carpenter's level on a stepladder leveled at the shoreline height. Sight down the edge and swing the level around, following the waterline. As you mark the shore you may need to clear brush with an ax or a chain saw. Do not leave sharp stumps that could later puncture the backhoe tires.

The backhoe is the pond maker's bionic arm. In an hour or so you can unearth just about all there is to know about a pond, short of digging it. If the site fails the pit tests, it's simple to refill the holes. Skip the testing, and you may wind up refilling the whole pond. Test holes should be excavated at random from the center of the pond basin to the shoreline. If the soil in the pond site

seems uniform, three or four pits may be sufficient. The greater the terrain varies, the more the test pits. For dammed ponds, don't forget to dig where the dam will be constructed. If the auger or the backhoe hits shallow ledge, reposition the dam or move the pond. Dams on ledge like to unplug ponds.

As the backhoe digs, watch the earth being wormed out of the ground. You will see layers of earth: the soil "profile." The backhoe should separate the top six-to-eight inches of topsoil from the rest of the material. Later, this rich topsoil can nourish your shoreland. Up next is the subsoil. If you hit deep heavy soil thick with clay, you have pond maker's gold. In the northeast area of the country, where clay-rich podzol soils are common, there's plenty of opportunity to strike it rich. Beware of limestone and sandstone, too permeable to hold water.

Watch for water while the backhoe cuts into the ground. If the vein is strong, water will quickly break through the punctured earth and bleed into the test pit. On flat terrain the test pit will eventually fill to the level of your water table. Such a pit is virtually a miniature dugout pond. Its water level will be the same as that of the finished pond; additional excavation will simply enlarge the storage capacity.

So far, test pits have steered you away from ledge and shale and helped meter soil and water. If you tapped clay-rich soil and a good flow of water, you have a pond site. At this point it helps to refine the pond shoreline. Using the test pits as guides, restake the pond to exclude ledge or unsuitably porous terrain. Maximize space where water is abundant. On a sloping site where a dammed pond is planned, be sure to reserve space about 30 feet wide on the downstream shoreline for dam construction.

Storage Capacity

Now your pond can be evaluated for storage capacity. Knowing a pond's potential water volume enables you to mesh the pond size with the watershed, and thus determine the pond's potential for auxillary use: irrigation, hydropower, aquaculture, and fire protection. The storage capacity of a pond is usually counted in acre-feet, 325,851 gallons per acre-foot. To reckon acre-footage, first compute the surface area of the pond. At regular intervals, measure the width and length of the staked shoreline. Plot the shoreline on graph paper and add up the squares to figure surface acreage. One acre is 43,560 square feet. Next estimate the maximum water depth and multiply by 0.4. The result, multiplied by surface acreage, yields acre-footage. For instance a pond of one-half acre with a maximum depth of ten feet holds two acre-feet, or 651,702 gallons. (The acre-footage formula averages the depth of all ponds at a uniform 40 percent of maximum.)

Knowing the storage capacity of the pond site, along with the size of the watershed, enables you to forecast reservoir-runoff compatibility. If you haven't figured your watershed size using SCS maps and photographs, mark the pond site on an USGS quadrangle map. Trace the contours of the area that drains into the site. With the 7½ inch scale, each ¼ inch square on the map represents 10 acres of land; with the 15 inch, each ¼ inch square is 40 acres.

In the prime pond making country east of the Mississippi and in the Northwest, this rough rule of thumb determines the ratio of watershed acreage/ground cover to pond capacity: each acre-foot of pond should receive runoff from territory no larger than two acres, if the ground cover is all woods or brush. If the ground cover is pasture, the drainage area should not exceed 1.5 acres for each acre of pond. If the drainage area is cultivated land, each acre-foot should receive runoff from no more than one acre. If the watershed is mixed, reckon accordingly.

Natural ponds form without need of formulas, of course. All these figures are approximations. I have had success overloading a pond with ten times more runoff than indicated. Overloading helps keep the pond fresh and full. But it won't work without tight watershed soils, a sturdy spillway, and, in the case of dammed ponds, a hefty embankment. By far, the worse mismatch occurs where the watershed falls short of supplying the pond. It's worth a few hours of mapping and math to make sure the pond site won't leave you dry.

Water For Crops & Livestock

Calculating your pond's storage potential helps determine its capacity for watering livestock and crops.

How much water will you need for irrigation? Water requirements vary with locale, soil condition, and crop; but a healthy ration of rain usually ranges from 1 to 2 inches of water per week through the principle growing season. That translates into about 28,000 gallons of water per acre, or 600 gallons for every 1000 square feet. A one acre-foot pond is likely to supply enough water to maintain this liquid diet without depleting the pond or bothering fish. Larger irrigation schemes that tap 10 percent or more of the pond volume require a steady resupply of water. To be sure that the inflow is adequate, dam up your spring, pipe the inflow into a bucket, and clock the time that it takes to fill. For instance, if a five-gallon bucket fills in two minutes, your pond will take in 25,200

gallons a week, regardless of precipitation. That's enough to keep a good sized garden and pond well-watered. If your pond is already built, measure the overflow to calculate surplus. Either way, do your figuring during drought season, when irrigation will be most needed and springs low.

A pond can be tapped for irrigation in many ways. A manual or motorized pump can move water to a storage container near the garden for manual watering or, better still, above the garden on a slope or platform, for gravity feed delivery. The pond can be the source for spraying, either motorized or manual. Backpack spray tanks designed for foliar feeding, crop spraying, or firefighting make fine watering devices. Small wind pumps will move 30 gallons per hour in winds over 7 mph; the Sparco windmill, for example, lifts water 13 feet over a horizontal distance of 30 feet. If the pond lies below the garden, with sufficient additional slope further below, hydraulic rams will deliver irrigation running on waterpower.

Drip irrigation is the most conservative watering technique. Water is piped to the edge of the garden, with a shut-off valve coupled where the drip system begins. By minimizing losses to vaporization, runoff, and deep seepage, a drip system cuts in half the need for irrigation. The most conservative use of the drip system results from small daily waterings. However, weekly irrigation encourages root growth and produces the strongest plants. One way or the other, avoid drenching crops to conserve minerals and nitrogen.

Besides supplying irrigation for gardens and orchards, a pond often creates a paddy in the spillway area that will support crops with heavy thirsts, like celery and watercress.

Livestock Water

To get an idea of your animal watering potential, balance storage capacity against needs.

Livestock Water Consumption

Cattle	9 to 18 gallons per day.
Dairy Cows	8 gallons per day plus ⅓ gallon for every pound of milk given. Up to 35 gallons per cow for drinking and barn needs.
Horse or Mule	8 to 12 gallons per day.
Sheep	1 to 3 gallons per day.
Laying Hens	8 gallons per day, per hundred.
Turkeys	10 to 15 gallons per day, per hundred.
Rabbits	1 gallon per day, per dozen.
Pig	1 to 3 gallons per day.

Ponds intended exclusively for livestock should be available in each pasture or grazing field, spaced about a quarter-mile apart in rough terrain, and no more than one mile apart in level areas. This spacing encourages uniform grazing. Ponds designed for both stock watering and recreation should be fenced so that the shoreline will not be trampled and the water muddied. The pond can be fenced completely, and stock water delivered by gravity pressure or pump. Otherwise, the pond can be partially enclosed, leaving a small area of the shore open to animals. Limited access works best in ponds with earth spillways. The access is located close to the outlet channel, so the current naturally flushes mud and manure from the pond. This system works best for waterfowl, chickens, and other lightweight critters. Heavier stock can quickly shred the turf and clog drainage ditches, especially during wet weather. Ponds intended exclusively for stock need not be expensive. In a few hours, a backhoe can excavate a small dugout that makes a fine waterhole or a habitat for waterfowl.

Excavation

Before machines lightened the work of clearing and excavating, stream impoundments were the most popular manmade reservoirs. The shore was simply skinned at the waterline where the dam would be notched into the banks. Later, excavated ponds were built with animals pulling plows, harrows, scrapers, and stumps. Labor was kept to a minimum by careful selection of terrain. Sites were chosen in open hollows with tight soil and good water prospects, where a minimum of stump removal and deep digging was needed. If the excavated earth could be used to build the dam, the site was considered especially promising. Trees that had to be removed were chopped and cleared from the area, roots and all. Sometimes cleared brush was piled aside, later to be heaped along the shoreline of the embankment, cinched in by a submerged fence. These brush liners were thought to prevent erosion along new dams whipped by choppy water.

After the pond maker had cleared the site, he brought in horsedrawn plows to carve up slabs of sod throughout the basin. These were saved to be grafted later to the raw land around the pond. Then the site was harrowed and scraped to hollow it out.

If an earth dam was planned, the foundation was carefully prepared to insure a seamless bond between the foundation ground and the earthfill embankment. A center line ditch was plowed out, topped with a foot or two of impervious soil, and packed by tramping animals. The ditch was then filled with a foot or two of earth and packed again.

Most pond makers shunned bedrock foundations because of the difficulty of creating a watertight seal between stone and earth. But given the choice of a ledge-based dam or no pond at all, stubborn pond makers worked to scrape the earth off the rock and carve a one-foot notch down the dam's base center line. The notch was covered with a reinforced cement wall, one or two feet high. On top of that the dam was raised. As the embankment was mounded and packed, supply pipes for barn or household water were laid in at levels below the frost line and covered with earth. Finally the draft animals were led around the excavation, tramping and packing. This was doubly effective when coordinated with rising pond water. As the basin filled, the animals were led in a spiral around the ascending waterline, packing it tight. This concluding step spanned the period it took the pond to fill, often several weeks. If the basin material was not naturally watertight, hay was spread around the reservoir and tramped in. Manure might then be added and packed in to help tighten the seal. Sometimes grass was seeded in the unfilled pond, and a herd of animals turned into graze. The basin developed a watertight glaze under their hooves. The pond maker who had set aside slabs of sod had several options when the excavation was complete. He could graft the turf onto the basin whenever the earth was too porous, or onto the embankment to prevent erosion. Sod was especially desirable along the leeward waterline of a large pond exposed to strong winds. To prevent erosion at the waterline, pond makers often lapped the sod shingle fashion. A word of caution: These traditional sealing techniques nourished warmwater fish ponds, but large doses of manure and organic matter didn't help trout.

Machines

The current popularity of ponds is due largely to big earth-moving machines. Hydraulic power speeds excavation, of course; but it's the tracks and tremendous weight that add the finishing touch—super-tight compaction of the basin and dam.

As the form of the pond varies, so does the pond-making machine. Big dugouts in wet terrain are usually scooped out by dragline excavator. Smaller dugouts can be built with a dragline or backhoe. Most dugouts require backup support from a bulldozer to spread and pack the earth. Dammed ponds can be built from start to finish with a single bulldozer.

Dugouts

The place to learn the basics of pond excavation is in a dugout. The principles of construction are primitive: for every scoop of earth removed you get a scoop of water, and there are no dams to build. As one contractor told me, "Dugouts? Hell, you can build them just about anyway you please!"

Because every gallon of water must be gained by excavation, big dugouts get expensive. But a modest one can be carved in a few days, or a few hours. Small-scale dugouts make thrifty fish ponds and greenhouse heat sinks.

Dugouts are popular with commercial fish farmers who grow warmwater fish in the South and Midwest, where clusters of small dugouts can be better managed than one big pond. In the grain belt, farmers are beginning to carve fields into dugouts where they produce fish more efficiently than corn or wheat. Cattlemen in the West excavate dugouts to make waterholes for ranging stock. Dugouts can be carved deep, with a small surface area, to conserve water more efficiently than shallower embankment ponds—an advantage where evaporation is a problem.

A dugout can be supplied with water in two ways. The simplest arrangement is to site the pond in a broad drainage way where it will fill naturally. Otherwise, offset dugouts are carved near a water source, preferably downhill; water is channeled in by a pipe or a ditch. The source may be anything from well water to runoff from a roof catch.

Earth is the main crop of dugout excavation. Usually the earth is spread over the land bordering the pond. A garden or a beach can be landscaped around the northern shore of the pond to catch lots of sunlight. Be careful to keep garden manure from leeching into the pond, unless you plan to raise a crop of algae for warmwater fish; trout do not appreciate a pond full of plankton.

I watched the earth from one large dugout spread over surrounding swampland to make a hayfield. As the basin was excavated, a dragline dumped earth into trucks that shuttled back and forth from the emerging field. When the dugout pond was done, three acres of fertile ground surrounded it.

To achieve tight adhesion between the surface and the new terrain, the land should first be prepared by removing roots and large stones. Some pond makers plow and harrow before applying fill. Others remove the topsoil completely with a bulldozer before adding more soil.

Often, the excavated earth from a dugout is used to build barriers to deflect water, wind, or snow. For

instance, barn runoff or silty ground flow can be channeled away from a pond with a berm or a gutter of earth built from the excavated diggings. Cattle waterholes on western rangelands are built to stand protected in the lee of earth mounds that defect snow and wind. These deflectors are built about ten feet back from the pond shore to prevent crushing of the banks, with gradual slopes to prevent slumping. Earth heaps of any kind should not be built just upstream from the dugout, where they can wash into the pond.

Although a dugout can be excavated in wet terrain by dragline, the diggings may be too wet to spread immediately. Some dugout builders prefer to muck out wet sites in the fall and let the earth dry over the winter. The pond is finished off the following spring. For finish grading, the best landscaping tool is a lightweight dozer.

While landscaping the dugout, be sure not to elevate the banks more than three or four feet high. Too much rim around the pond creates a crater and invites erosion and trouble with access. Keep in mind that fill will settle. Earth that is dozer-packed may settle up to five percent of its depth; unpacked, it may settle as much as ten percent.

Excavation

Once your dugout site is cleared, stake the pond at intervals of fifty feet or less. Check with a level to make sure the dugout basin is on an even footing. There should be no more than a foot or two of slope. Otherwise, excavation will create enormous banks on the upstream end. No matter how hard you try, water will not tilt. A sloping site calls for an embankment pond, not a dugout.

Look over the staked pond site and satisfy yourself that the dugout is not boxed in too tightly by the terrain. In a rich watershed you may want to enlarge the pond later, or

add additional ones. Supplementary dugouts sometimes are excavated near a large pond; a small downstream dugout makes a good habitat for waterfowl and warmwater fish, critters that you may not want in the main pond. Upstream dugouts can be used to settle out sediment before it flows into the main pond.

When you are satisfied with the shape, size, and position of the dugout, mark the shoreline stakes with the depth of excavation and the angle of the basin slopes to guide your equipment operator. The deeper the dugout, the greater the storage capacity, the longer the lifespan, and the higher the price. Minimum depth is about four to five feet. Shallower, it is likely to sprout weeds and freeze fish. However, shallow dugouts can be used for aquadomes, sauna baths, fire ponds, irrigation, livestock water, etc.

Dugout banks can be cut at a rather steep angle, about 2:1, because there is no dam to slump—and because draglines and backhoes cut a steeper wall than a bulldozer. Steep banks increase storage space and discourage weeds. Do not cut the slopes any steeper than 2:1 unless you reinforce the basin. In fact, you might want to grade one bank at a gradual 3 or 4:1 slope to make a beach or a ramp for watering animals.

Contractors

Booking an earth-moving machine is like booking a fishing trip: it's the captain's ship but your charter. Choose an experienced contractor you trust, with equipment that suits your plans and budget. Don't let the intimidating roar of the bulldozer drown out your questions or suggestions.

If you are planning to build a small dugout, a backhoe makes a thrifty precision digger. This hydraulic scoop is

about the cheapest power shovel available. Because of its short reach, the backhoe is most efficient at carving ponds 10 to 20 feet in diameter or long, narrow lagoons or raceways.

A circular dugout of larger storage capacity requires larger equipment. In a site that is not swamped, the best all-around machine is a bulldozer. Unlike other heavy equipment, a bulldozer is capable of making a pond from start to finish: clearing topsoil, cuffing out rocks and roots, carving the basin, installing pipe, and spreading earth over the shore. Bulldozers can excavate up to 1200 yards of earth in a day.

If the basin is badly drenched, the earth will be too heavy for the machine to move. All the horsepower in the world is worthless if the machine sinks, so timing is a critical factor. The best bet for success with a bulldozer in a dugout is during the driest season of the year, in a site flanking the main flow of water, to be fed by side pipe or a ditch.

To keep the basin drained during excavation, pond builders sometimes dig a ditch leading out of the downstream area of the basin or bail out water with a pump, or both. This can put a hole in your budget because it may double excavation time and cost for the machinery.

Where drainage problems threaten to swamp the bulldozer and your budget, the dragline is the best tool for a dugout. The dragline succeeds where bulldozers disappear because it works from outside the pond basin, perched on solid ground or a portable platform of planks or steel. A dragline can yank out roots and stones, scrape ledge clean, hoist pipe, and dredge soggy earth. This makes it ideal for restoring old ponds, as well as digging fresh ones. However, a dragline cannot clear topsoil, pack a pond basin, or grade landscape.

The dragline operator usually begins a dugout by digging a ditch through the middle of the site to drain water. Then, working from the middle of the basin back to the shoreline, he scoops out the earth and dumps it on the banks to dry and later to be spread on the landscape. In some sites pumping may be necessary, especially after heavy rain or work layoffs.

In theory, a dragline could build a pond of unlimited size by moving back earth from the site continuously, but the cost of handling the earth over and over again grows with the size of the pond. With its reach of about 45 feet, the dragline can most practically dig a pond about 90 feet wide. On larger dugouts a bulldozer must accompany the dragline to help with earth removal. A dragline can excavate roughly 900 yards of earth a day.

Dug & Dammed Ponds

Sloping terrain makes dugout excavation impractical, so pond makers build embankments of earth to hold water. By raising a dam on a hill, across a draw, or around the downstream end of a sloping hollow, the builder fills in the missing rim of an earth bowl. When the dam tops the level of the planned upstream shoreline, the pond is complete.

The amount of excavation needed to create a dug-and-dammed pond will vary depending on the terrain and the storage capacity desired. In a good pond site—a sloping hollow—excavation and embankment construction should be swift. If the pond site is on a steep hill that lacks natural enclosing flanks, substantial yardage must be dug from the basin and moved to the embankment. A neighbor had to carve a 16-foot deep pond because he needed so much earth to complete his dam. The earth from my 8-foot deep pond, on a more gradual slope, provided

enough fill to complete my dam.

Since the upstream slope of the pond site contributes roughly half of the bowl at the outset, the pond maker must complete the enclosure by raising the rim around the lower end. A veteran pond maker will often plan the dam in his head, tramping around the site and eyeballing the slope, and then build the pond without pounding a single stake. On the other hand, Soil Conservation Service agents usually stake the site, calculate elevations every fifty feet, and draw up scale models of the pond, dam, and surrounding terrain. I think it's best to compromise: plan the dam with a few dozen stakes and a transit or level.

Site the dam first by setting up a transit or a level inside the pond basin. Level it at about two feet above the desired upstream shoreline, giving you the necessary freeboard. Now swing the sight downstream until the land first drops out of view, and mark the spot. There the dam will butt into the slope. Continue to sight across the downstream end of the pond, tracing the top of your imaginary dam, until you again sight land. Mark the spot. Now you have fixed the two points where the embankment will tie into the land. Between these marks you will build the dam.

You may want an embankment that runs fairly straight across the slope or one that curves. On a steep slope it may prove too costly to run the dam out very far. But on a gradual slope you may be able to impound a large reservoir with a long, curving, shallow dam. The difference in elevation across the pond site determines the height of the dam. For example, if the downstream edge of the site lies six feet below the upstream shoreline and you add a couple of feet for freeboard, an 8-foot dam is required.

Foundation work for the dam involves clearing topsoil, boulders, and stumps from the dam base area. The earth beneath the dam must be tested to judge its ability to fulfill its double function: holding up the dam structure and holding in the water. Test pits in the embankment area will enable you to judge the quality of the ground base. The best ground base is a mixture of watertight clays and silts, with some sand and gravel. Bedrock or ledge in the base area may contain water-draining fissures and prevent a good seal between the ground and the dam, and should be avoided.

Ground with an excess of sand and gravel makes poor material for the dam base. Pond makers in Vermont often remedy sandy sites by digging a center-line core trench in the dam base and packing it with watertight clay-rich soil, carved from the pond basin or elsewhere. This core trench is usually cut 3 to 6 feet wide and 1 to 2 feet deep. If the pond maker can dig through the sand into a clay or silt layer, so much the better. After the watertight material is packed into the core trench, the embankment is raised.

A swampy base of silt and clay also requires special foundation work. Clay and silt hold water, but in excess make a weak base, which can cause the dam to slump. This is remedied by enlarging the base of the foundation and flattening the embankment slopes inside and out.

The dam for my pond was based on swampy clay and silt, so it was built 60 feet wide at the base and 20 feet wide on the top. That helped distribute the load over a large area. In some swampy dam sites, pond makers cut core trenches similar to those used in sandy sites. Spongy organic material is removed and replaced with a clay-silt-sand mixture or concrete.

A basin that consists of good impervious pond material will usually yield earthfill satisfactory for the dam itself. Material containing about 20 percent clay, without too

much sand, gravel, or organic matter, is best. An excess of either sand-gravel or silt-clay will weaken the dam. Where sand and gravel make up a large portion of the earthfill, pond makers build a core of clay-rich earth throughout the dam to prevent leakage. Clay-rich material can sometimes be scooped up from select areas of the excavation for this inner core. To help waterproof the dam, the embankment is built wide, with 3: 1 slopes. Pond makers caution against using embankment fill composed of organic silt or pure clay. These materials hold water, but they make poor dam material. The organic matter will decompose, while the clay is liable to dry and crack.

When the makeup of the foundation base and the earthfill has been determined, you can choose your dam location and stake it out. Begin by staking out the center line of the dam every 25 feet or so, using markers tall enough to top the dam surface. Peg the inside and outside lines of the dam to completely trace the base size. The base area is generally about three times as wide as the top. For instance, an embankment with a top surface 10 feet wide, just big enough for tractors, trucks, and barbeques, needs a 30 foot base, so lines pegged about 15 feet on either side of the center line mark its foundation.

Once you see the rough shape of the dam you can consider the spillway site. The spillway should be located where it can exhaust water directly over the top of the dam and down into a suitable water channel, already established by groundwater flow. You don't want to run overflow down your driveway, or straight into your garden. The spillway area of the dam is one place you don't skimp: it must be tough. Spillways are often placed on the seam where the dam ties into the natural terrain. (See Spillways.)

The natural flow of the bulldozer is downhill, scooping up earth and pushing it across the site to the dam. Sometimes topsoil and debris are pushed to the extreme edge of the embankment foundation and buried under the rising dam. This organic material must be built into the far outside of the core structure of the dam, where it can decay without opening up leaks. Large boulders should be excluded from the embankment. They may be pushed off to the flanks of the site and later retrieved for diving headstones and fish shelters. As the excavation deepens, water will begin to flow into the basin. If pooling water threatens to bog down the machine, a drainage ditch may be required. The builder's final task will be to put in the plug by filling the ditch.

Spillways

The Perils of Piping

The new thirst for ponds reminds me of the beginning of the wood heat renaissance a decade ago: lots of trial and error. Pond makers today are chalking up mistakes at about the same rate that wood burners did. Most of the wasted time and money is going down the drain through underground spillways. It's time for land users to take a new look at the open sesame of pondmaking: piping.

Some background first. Earth ponds flow naturally toward oblivion. Vegetation decays, sediment accumulates, and the basin erodes. Eventually, without help, the pond disappears. Pond keepers resist decay in several ways. Inflows of water are maintained to reduce silt and sediment. Unwanted aquatic growth is discouraged with deep-dug, steep-sided basins and annual drawdowns. And the reservoir is designed to withstand the abrasive force of overflowing water. It is this effort to exhaust overflow without damaging the earth structure that constitutes the main line of defense.

I recently revisited a couple of ponds that I watched being carved last year, one in New Hampshire and one in Vermont. Both had been sited to catch ample runoff and spring water. Both were sidehill dug-and-dammed ponds. And both covered about a quarter-acre surface, plunging to ten feet at the deepest. In fact, these two ponds mirrored each other across the Connecticut River, with one big difference: the New Hampshire pond was fitted with an underground drain coupled to a standpipe, while the Vermont pond was designed to expell surplus water over a simple spillway across the embankment. Two steady streams of water leaked from the New Hampshire pond, one through the tar-covered 8″ corrugated steel drain, the other seeping out just beneath the pipe. Its water level was three feet below the standpipe opening, despite rich spring rains that had saturated the earth and topped off neighboring ponds. In Vermont, the simpler earth pond brimmed full. Surplus water overflowed smoothly down the riprap-lined channel. No piping, no leaks. The excavation price for each pond was about $2000; but with the addition of pipe, the total for the New Hampshire pond had risen substantially.

"What's the price of pipe now?" I asked Leonard Cook, a Norwich, Vermont, pond builder. He laughed. "No one knows! It changes everyday!" But he guessed that the materials for the T-riser system in the New Hampshire pond had cost about $500. Adding labor and bulldozer costs, we figured that the piping had added at least $1000 to the cost of the leaky pond.

Despite the pitfalls, it's not hard to fathom the lure of pond plumbing. A bottom drain offers the potential for kitchen-faucet control of the reservoir: fast flushing for fish harvests and habitat changes, and push-button drawdowns to quell unwanted shoreline growth. And some say that winter fishkills in North Country ponds can be stopped by piping out the lower layer of water, which may grow fatally oxygen-lean under ice and snow. Add a standpipe to the underground drain and the pond keeper's mastery seems complete; a vertical pipe lopped off at the desired level promises to maintain a steady waterline—*if* the incoming water is sufficient. And in small ponds fed by mammoth watersheds, heavy overflow through a standpipe may be preferable to stressing an overland spillway. Yet, like the New Hampshire pond keeper who is having his pipe system sealed with concrete and replaced by an embankment spillway, many people find themselves badly served by subterranean plumbing.

How come? The basic problem is poor design integrity. Earth and steel don't mix. The whole system is aching to leak, and the pond maker's first occasion to use the drain is usually to fix it. Easier said than done. The drain plug probably lies buried in sediment at the bottom of the pond. Experienced builders know that the tightest plug is a simple softwood stopper hewed and stuffed into the underwater end of the pipe, and the uncorking action is a strong punch with a long pipe applied from the outside. Of course, once the plug is smashed out, there's no closing it. So much for push-button control. The notion of maintaining a perfect water level is often another fantasy. In many ponds the standpipe pokes up like the periscope on a stray submarine because the inflow is not rich enough to produce a constant surplus. Or, even more likely, because the pipe leaks.

Usually two kinds of drain pipe are favored: culvert-style steel or iron. Steel pipe is available in lengths that can be trucked to the pond site and then bolted together. Yet, unless pond makers are careful to use tar-coated, double-riveted spiral pipe, spot-welded in the trench, they may soon find a leak squirting through the seams. Iron pipe from a scrapyard is thriftier. But because several pieces usually must be welded together to gain sufficient length, careful installation is crucial. Without a solid base and good earth packing, settling movements can break the joints. If an overflow standpipe is coupled to the drain, the drainpipe must be tilted slightly downward to get a clean flow and to prevent sediment from clogging the way. Eight to twelve-inch stock is favored for small ponds.

Siting the drain is tricky. Pond makers must anticipate the main inflow of water and locate the pipe safely beyond the turbulence. I saw one job take a costly detour when the drainage ditch had to be refilled and carved in a new location because the main vein of spring water splashed too close to the planned outlet. The builder knew that silt soon would bury the drain.

Most frustrating of all is the potential for leakage from a perfectly sealed drain or standpipe system. At 62 pounds per cubic foot, pond water has a powerful tendency to squirt out around the exterior of the buried pipe. Pond makers who install pipe work to overcome this by ringing the outside of the pipe with anti-seep collars. These fittings clasp tightly to the pipe like nuts on a bolt, welded or clamped at intervals of about ten feet. Good pond makers shudder at the thought of installing pipe without anti-seep collars. Yet they admit that collars are no guarantee against leakage. A pipe in the pond basin is like a splinter that never goes away.

Considering the high cost and failure rate of pond piping, it's not surprising that pond makers increasingly recommend a roll of hose for siphoning. Right now the Department of Agriculture is at work on a flexible-hose spillway system designed to snake up from the bottom of the pond basin, cross the shore, and then overflow. In addition to side-stepping the obstacles inherent in underground piping, this hose drains low-strata, high-sediment water rather than skimming the clear upper layer, as does a standpipe or natural spillway. Hence pond eutrophication will be slowed.

Earth Spillways

I put down all this piping business as a prelude to viewing earth spillways, which I find far superior to subterranean piping in ponds suitably matched to their watersheds.

A good earth spillway keeps a pond overflowing smoothly when inflow creates a surplus. Otherwise, the spillway takes a rest. No standpipe poking up in the air. No seeps. For a pond that overflows only during heavy rains or thaws, a riprapped earth spillway near the downstream end of the pond usually is adequate. Common-sense conservation methods make the best spillway foundation: avoid erodible soils and prevent debris from clotting the channel. The greater the overflow, the tougher the spillway must be to resist erosion. In Vermont, granite slabs or concrete will be found lining especially hardworking spillways. A simple grassy channel, however, can be sufficient to carry off overflow from a dugout pond. If the downstream area where the spillway will discharge has been disturbed by excavation, the vegetative cover can be reestablished while the pond fills.

The spillway for an embankment pond is carved by bulldozer (or shovel) at the conclusion of construction, deep enough to guarantee two or three feet of banking above the high-water mark. Such a spillway is often located at the end of the dam where the embankment is spliced to the natural slope. This area is a good site for the overflow since the upstream hillside provides a natural stronghold against erosion. Of the two seams where dam and hillside meet, the spillway should be laid where the overflow will best stream away without eroding the embankment structure.

Spillways are divided into three sections: the approach channel, the control section, and the exit slope. The *approach channel* is an extension of the slope of the pond basin leading out of the pond. The slope angle should be inclined back into the pond at an angle of at least two or three degrees so that water will drain clean back into the reservoir. Good drainage means fewer mosquitos. Make the approach at least twice as wide as the control section. The *control section,* or crest, is the level channel that runs through the embankment about one to three feet below the embankment rim. This channel should be located on the upstream side of the midpoint of the embankment, anywhere from two to ten feet wide, and at least ten feet long. The longer the control section, the better its ability to handle overflow. A turn in the control section is permissible, but be sure the sweep is slow and easy. No abrupt angles. To help buffer erosion, the spillway control section should be reinforced with a riprap of stones about three inches in diameter. These may be culled from the raw new embankment or imported. Otherwise, bricks or a mix of concrete and stones can be applied. I would avoid treated wood because of possible water contamination. Culvert pipe—whole or cut in half lengthwise—makes an unreliable liner since water tends to work out underneath, especially after frost heaving. The banks of the spillway control section should be mulched to protect against erosion, and vegetation reestablished. Spillway side slopes should be moderate, no steeper than three to one, to prevent slumping.

The *exit channel* should drain overflow away from the pond without damaging the downstream slope of the embankment. The exit channel will drop off at about the same angle as the outside of the dam. Like the control section, it should be lined with stones or other reinforcement and maintained with conservation tactics. Wing dykes sometimes are used to protect the embankment.

Water should be carried far enough below the dam to prevent any washing back or eddying that might cause damage in a flood.

The Pond Keeper's Seasons

"Ponds need no such labor and charges as other commodities do." That was how the elder Pliny saw the need of pond maintenance nineteen centuries ago, and it's a view that still looks good, especially to husbanders of land-based labor-intensive farming schemes. To many of them, pond culture has all the lure of a forever-standing *Gone Fishin'* sign. Yet anyone who's tended a pond knows the periodic chores: erosion and weed control, spillway repair, cleanup, and most vexing, plugging leaks. The pond keeper who neglects them imperils fish, water, pond, and the neighbors downstream. If, indeed, pond culture requires less labor than most country endeavors, the reason has more to do with the pond keeper than with the pond itself—for the cunning pond keeper works with the seasons, synchronizing chores with the life cycle of the pond and tapping the forces of nature for support.

Winter

The advantages of pond keeping by the season are most dramatic in the winter. The very existence of some ponds depends on it. Across town, tucked behind the Strafford meeting house, sits a small, flat field. For more than forty summers it has been Elwin Coburn's potato patch. And every winter it is transformed. Village firemen spray down sheets of ice and put out a winter skating pond.

It's the transformation of water into a crystalline platform that makes winter magic for pond keeping. For instance, why measure surface acreage in summer? Throwing soggy lines around the shoreland seems off the mark when it's so simple to stand on ice and pace the feet in snow.

The sand drop is another well-esteemed pond keeper's trick that takes advantage of the ice deck. It's an upkeep technique well suited to older ponds in need of restoration, particularly where aquatic vegetation or mud gets unruly. To set up a sand drop, the pond keeper spreads a two-to-four inch layer of sand—*not* salted road sand—over the ice. In spring when the ice thaws, *poof!* The sand falls in a uniform layer over the basin floor. Sand works like an inorganic mulch, shading out weeds and, like the finings in a beer crock, holding down sediment. In muddy ponds, it's a good carpet material for the basin floor. One of my neighbors was able to use a sand drop to eliminate the slimy bottom in her family's pond, along with snakes and leeches. True, the sand drop does fill in the pond to a minute degree, but it's not often done, and it sure beats herbicides.

The sand drop technique works well for depositing boulders in the pond. Stones falling into the center of the basin can provide a shady retreat for fish. Or they can be arranged to create a diving rock, a foundation for a pier or platform, or an island, welcomed by waterfowl where dogs are a bother.

It seems natural to extend the drop technique to include lime, fertilizer, or precipitating agents, sometimes used by pond keepers as a tonic for ailing waters. Beware that these ingredients are not flushed out of the pond with spring runoff. Concentrate the drop upstream, away from the spillway area.

Icing can mean trouble, too. Late in autumn when my pond begins to freeze, I watch the frothy inflow harden into a starry glaze, like a miniature Milky Way. Those stars are bubbles of air caught in the ice, and they signal the start of a spell of lowered oxygen levels in the water, potentially fatal for fish.

The trout here need about five parts per million dissolved oxygen in winter; other fish that winter over under ice have similar requirements. All may be subject to oxygen starvation due to overcrowding, underwater vegetation decay, and lack of light to stimulate photosynthesis. So far I've never experienced any winterkills, and my stock has climbed to a winter peak of 60 eight-inch brook trout—not bad for an eighth-acre pond with no supplemental feed. Proper pond construction accounts for most of my successful defense against winter oxygen starvation. At least five feet of water under the ice is recommended in these North Country parts. Besides, the pond is too young for a massive vegetation die-off. But there's another reason that ice hasn't choked the trout: broom hockey. Keeping a patch of ice clear for skating opens up the bottom of the pond to the sunlight necessary for oxygen production in submerged plants.

The pond keeper can also turn to the wind for help with aeration. Given at least a two-mph breeze, a Pondmaster water circulator will stir a hole in the ice and aerate the water. The Pondmaster and another larger wind-powered water circulator, the Lake Aid, are touted as year-round aerators, though I wouldn't count on much of a breeze in summer when oxygen levels are lowest. For summer aeration, motor-driven aerators make the best insurance against fishkills.

In *A New Booke of Good Husbandry*, Bishop Dubravius recalls his hardest trial by ice. It was the Lenten carp harvest. The bishop's men had come to him complaining that the harvest was impossible. They had chopped a hole in the ice and lowered nets into the pond, but not a carp had stirred. Round and round the pond the men stampeded, trying to drive the fish into the nets. No luck. So the bishop took down a wagonload of earth to the pond. Opposite the hole his men had opened Dubravius cut again. Then he wheeled over his wagon and dumped the earth into the water. An explosive burst of earth embroiled the pond in clouds of silt, and the frightened carp fled straight into the nets. Amen.

Spring

The main spring maintenance objective is to be a good midwife at the rebirth of the pond after its long dark winter. The pond wants to take in big gulps of fresh, richly-aerated water and flush out last year's crud. You help. But beware: simultaneously the pond must be shielded against two threats that arrive with spring waters—erosion and silt.

The erosive, silting power of spring flood water is formidable. A stream that doubles its speed quadruples its load-carrying capacity. The more silt it carries, the greater its ability to erode. A vicious hydrologic cycle.

Moreover, at the same time that thawing snow and falling rain are adding to spring floodwaters, the shoreland heaves around as frost works its way out of the ground. Spillways, ditches, and berms are undermined. Piping cracks and trashracks clog. In a few weeks of spring the pond is likely to suffer more damage than all the rest of the year.

As usual, good siting and construction make the best

Riprapping the inflow.

defense against reservoir wear and tear. In spring the wise pond keeper will congratulate himself for steering clear of big stream inflows; even a small intermittent vein can deliver an avalanche of silt.

Throughout spring, water channels leading into and out of the pond should be cleaned and reinforced. Debris in the vein feeding the pond will decay, eating up oxygen and tipping up water temperatures; debris in the spillway will back up overflowing water, causing erosion around the spillway approach channel and shore, not to mention the chance for flooding. Spring is also time to check for ice damage to piping.

Mind the watershed above the pond, especially cultivated farm land or terrain doused with manure, chemicals, or garbage. Open upstream land is prone to feeding detritus into ponds. Diversion ditches and berms around the upstream hemisphere of the pond help detour silt, but don't dig them in spring! Refrain, too, early in the year, from logging, road work, or construction in the near upstream watershed.

Pipes that feed stream water to bypass ponds often clog in spring. A "digger dam" in the stream just *above* the intake pool will usually sweep silt around the pipe, and in conjunction with a screen and/or trashrack, will keep the inflow clear. (See *Digger Pond* chapter.) For clearest passage through rough spring waters, some pond keepers find it simplest to close off side pipes at the source.

In the book *Aquaculture,* authors Bardach, Ryther, and McClarney recommend keeping silt out of fish ponds with a "saran" filter, a plastic mesh kin to today's grain sack material. For ponds fed by sidepipe, they recommend capping the outlet with a saran sock, kind of a pond condom. For ponds with a natural channel feed, they suggest trapping silt in a saran-bottomed box at shoreline water level. Not a bad notion, especially where fish—or fish keepers—are vexed by especially silty waters.

Yet here in a forest watershed of tight-knit soils, my pond needs no filter. Besides, from the foot of the inflow I like to dive into the water, not into a box. So in spring I use an old logger's trick for clearing roughed-up streams. I lay a hay bale crossways in the channel to filter out silt. Later, when the water warms up, I shovel out a wheelbarrow or two of spring silt, fine fill for the puddles that settled in the dam after excavation. The marsh marigolds that I planted in the inflow channel help hold the earth in place, too.

Stones cleared from the embankment after excavation become a thrifty resource, piled by the spillway for springtime repairs. This riprap can be paved in the inflow channel and along patches of muddy shore. Incidentally, rock paving is recommended both as an antidote for banks that erode under wind-whipped waves and as a barrier against fish poachers and pond unpluggers like otters and mink.

To finish off the rites of spring on a modern note, I suggest you look to that sulphurous bruise that appears on ponds thawing downwind of industrial smokestacks. All winter, the ice has been catching polluted snow and rain. When it melts, six months of accumulated acid rubbish sinks into the pond. It's a bad time to stock fish. Better wait a few weeks and let the pond flush. Those hockey clearings won't help much unless snow is moved off the pond, or at least as far as the spillway, where it will flush out quickly. Lime or wood ashes are a long-standing remedy for acid pH. Anywhere from 10 to 100 pounds of agricultural lime may be needed. It's best to test the water and correct in small doses. What's really needed, of course, is a dose of intelligence in high places.

Summer

Three typical problems come up in summer ponds: overgrowth of aquatic vegetation and algae, low water, and dead fish.

The emergence of aquatic vegetation and algae is just about inevitable in an earth pond. In fact, a certain amount of vegetation is fine nourishment, feeding oxygen to fish and other critters, and helps keep down sediment. For many warmwater fish, a bloom of algae means a rich pond. A healthy growth of algae is said to fade a bright object from sight beginning about 18 inches underwater. For trout farmers, the water should be clearer, say Chablis compared to Bordeaux.

Excess algae and weeds make an obvious mess of pond structure and water quality. Clouds of algae ground swimmers, tangle fishing lines, clog spillways and pipes, and lure animals you don't want. Massive vegetation will drive up water temperatures, stressing fish; eventually large masses of vegetation die off, exhausting the oxygen supply and contributing to fishkills.

Again, good construction is the best maintenance. A deep pond with steep banks discourages weeds and algae. It's important to keep up water levels to discourage weeds from getting a toehold on the banks and to keep up conservation tactics, especially ditching away runoff that could feed vegetation. Summer is the time to fix fences, too; keeping animals off the shoreland prevents trampling of the banks.

For conservation agents, summer brings a deluge of phone calls from pond owners maddened by weeds and algae. Often, callers are left with the impression that the only solution is a bottle of chemicals or a dredging machine. Copper sulphate, Cutrine Plus and, until it was banned, 2 4 D, are just a few of the herbicides that I have seen recommended by conservation agencies and aquaculture literature. Dyes that shade out the sun and kill vegetation are also popular. (Dragline dredging makes an effective non-chemical cleanup but may cost as much as a new pond.)

There are several reasons why I would hesitate to douse a pond with chemicals. Who really knows the long-term effects of these solutions? Many herbicides have been on the market a short time, and there is little to gain in making your pond a guinea pig for the chemical industry. I can't imagine dumping herbicides in my pond without tainting the food chain all the way from the May fly larvae in the mud to the drinking water in my neighbors' springs and wells downstream. In fact, most herbicides and pesticides are used by commercial fish growers who know that there are natural, albeit slower, cleanup techniques, but complain that in the rush for profits there's no time for anything but the quick chemical fix. Alas, these growers are just discovering that their chemicals are backfiring, causing off-flavors in pond fish. And there's no profit in that, no matter how quickly fish grow. So, lately, there's been talk about "dewatering." That's the current aquacultural lingo for Dubravius' favorite natural antiseptic: the drawdown.

By lowering the water level anywhere from a foot to fully empty, the pond keeper can kill off aquatic vegetation and parasites, and restore water clarity and oxygen levels. A siphon hose or a pump is the simplest means for a drawdown. In ponds with bottom drains, it may be difficult to manage anything less than complete draining, and that's not always necessary, especially if the problem is simply a patch of shoreline weeds. A full drawdown is out of the question for a pond carrying fish or irrigating a garden—unless the pond keeper has another pond and

Before drawdown

. . . and after.

can drawdown alternately.

During a drawdown the pond basin is exposed to the air and the sun, killing off algae and aquatic vegetation. Exposure to the elements also hastens decomposition of vegetation on the basin floor, leading to richer oxygen levels when the pond refills. A partial drawdown may occur naturally during hot and dry weather. The pond water level drops a foot or two without the pond keeper's lifting a finger. This is the time to step in with a shovel or sickle to clean up the banks. It's a good idea to cut or pull weeds before seeds form, but be sure your weeding doesn't coincide with fish spawning, when eggs may be incubating in the reeds.

The complete drawdown—fully drained and fallowed for the summer—spreads an antiseptic effect throughout the basin and enables the pond keeper to change the fish population and get at the rich muck. Dredgings make a good topsoil spread or garden amendment, as long as they are composted first. A friend of mine beefed up his sandy front yard with fresh pond scrapings and wound up with a lawn full of cattails. On a garden, fresh dredgings can burn plants.

In 1600, in England, John Taverner published a treatise on the art of pond culture and orcharding, *Certaine Experiments Concerning Fish and Fruits*. It's recognized as one of the first studies of husbandry in the West based on observation and experiment, rather than hearsay. Taverner recommended the drawdown as the ultimate pond cleanser. He summed up the effects of the drawdown:

"You shall avoid superfluous numbers of fish, which greatly hinder the growth and goodness of your greater fish. Secondly, by that means you shall so proportion your pond, that it shall never be overstored. Thirdly, by that means your water shall always be excellent sweet by reason it overfloweth such ground as hath taken the sun and ayre all sommer before."

Here in Orange County, I've watched several ponds clear up after summer-long drawdowns. The most dramatic was a small farm pond that had been neglected for years: clumps of algae clouded the surface, cattle trampled the banks, and pasture runoff leeched into the water. After fencing his cattle downstream from the watershed, the pond keeper siphoned out the water with three garden hoses and left the basin exposed to the sun for the summer. A year later, refilled and stocked with trout, the pond sparkled.

Fish, too, may be enlisted for pond maintenance. For instance, carp are used to keep the canals of Holland clean. Down in Arkansas, Jim Malone is renowned for the carp he raises to sell to pond keepers and waterway officials seeking non-toxic weed killers. One of his fish will down up to 10 pounds of algae, moss, and weeds in a year. Yet many pond keepers must do without the help of this thrifty pond sweep. Game fishermen have lobbied to outlaw the carp in all but 19 states: Hawaii, Alaska, Arkansas, Kentucky, Alabama, West Virginia, North and South Dakota, New Jersey, Mississippi, Montana, Colorado, Iowa, Rhode Island, Massachusetts, Maryland, Minnesota, Delaware, and Kansas. Fishermen argue that the carp muddies streams and displaces game fish. Besides, with all those bones it's just *too* hard to clean! Elsewhere, especially in Asia, the carp is a popular food with reputed medicinal powers. Korean women relish the fish for prenatal health.

When I discovered that carp are verboten in Vermont I

felt cheated. Must the pond keeper who can't take time out for a drawdown turn to chemicals?

Not at all, Jim Malone told me. "Don't take offense," he said, "but you should think of your trout as coldwater carp."

Malone is right. Trout have reputations as fussy feeders, picky as spoiled Siamese cats; yet for three years I've watched my brook trout gain weight without an ounce of supplemental feed. I see them feast on the bottom as much as in the air: the water is as transparent as an aquarium. I recalled my neighbor's drawdown and follow-up trout stocking: clearly, the fish were pitching in to keep it clean. And I recalled an old Vermont tradition: to keep the farmhouse water clean, a trout was dropped in the well.

Turbid water is another problem in summer ponds. It's not unusual for a pond to cloud up after heavy rain, new ponds especially. In certain soils, for instance in Oklahoma, soil particles resist settling because of an unusual electrical charge that keeps them ricocheting around. Ponds in these soils tend toward permanent turbidity. The effect can be damaging: turbid water reduces light penetration and photosynthesis, smothers bottom life, cuts waste assimilation, and impairs spawning. Some pond keepers recommend agricultural lime or gypsum to clear turbid waters, with dosages ranging from 10 to 100 pounds per surface acre. But before I'd go shopping for agricultural chemicals, I'd try hay. Pond keepers have found that strewing old hay around the shallows helps clear turbid water, roughly seven to ten bales per surface acre. Decaying organic matter apparently reduces Brownian movement in the soil, causing particles to clump and settle.

The half-empty pond is a traditional sign of pond fail-ure. Usually it's due to structural leakage or improper siting in dry terrain. Not that it's unusual for an earth pond to seep somewhat—only synthetic sealers or liners can make a pond truly watertight. What the pond keeper wants to prevent is *excessive* seepage. What's excessive? I knew one young lady whose new pond was a flop. At best in summer it held a couple of feet of muddy broth. Still, she was happy. "Honey, all I need is a place to roll around in the mud and I'm fine." Of course, commercial fish farmers can't afford that low tide effect, and I wouldn't welcome it either.

Besides, new ponds, embankment ponds especially, tend to get off to leaky starts. During the first summer or two, a new pond may never reach its designed water level. Freshly excavated ponds are like coffee filters. At first the liquid streams right through; then gradually settling sediment and the weight of the water tightens the seal, with some help from the settling shoreland and new vegetation. Of course, some ponds plainly fail. How can you tell? The neighbors' ponds are full.

Fixing low-tide ponds begins with a search for leakage. Ponds with piping often leak around the outside of the pipe or through seams, gaskets, and valves. In most cases, unless a fitting can be easily replaced, pipe repair involves digging up the line to repair joints or to implant anti-seep collars.

In embankment ponds, the seal between the ground base and the bottom of the dam is another spot to watch. Hence, the traditional emphasis on thorough clearing and preparation of the dam foundation ground, a wide base, and maybe a clay-filled center-line core trench. An extra half-hour of bulldozer compaction on the dam after construction also helps.

To Sherm Stebbins, the Randolph, Vermont, pond

maker, the most maddening cause of dam leakage is improper siting. He told me about a job during his early days as a pond maker.

"My clients were deadset on a site on top of a ledge," Sherm said. Too rocky, he advised. They wouldn't hear of it, so Sherm built the pond. Driving by one afternoon, Sherm saw a dark stain spreading across the embankment. He raced up to the house to warn the owners that their dam was crumbling. That night they drained the pond, and Sherm brought back his bulldozer to tear apart the embankment. He packed in a layer of clay over the rocky base and rebuilt the dam. The pond filled. Again it leaked. So they drained it, and Sherm once more tore apart the dam, added more clay and let it fill. This time the dam held. Sherm warned me, "Never, never put in a pond where you don't trust the earth!"

Porous soil in the pond basin is another cause of leakage. A technique for sealing porous soil is to drain the pond and layer the basin with clay or bentonite, packed in with a sheepsfoot roller or dozer. Be wary of "sealers." I've seen one pond sealer called "SS 13" make a piteous, polluted spectacle of a leaky pond, without plugging it a bit. Some pond keepers seal leaky basins with a plastic liner. The pond must be drained and lined with sand to cushion the plastic against puncture. Often, 20 mil plastic is spread over the basin, lapstreaked at the edges, and then covered with another few inches of sand.

Sometimes the best solution for low-level ponds is more water. I watched one low pond fill up with a supplement of water from a specially dug well. Another was revived when the owner tapped an upstream brook with one hundred yards of four-inch PVC pipe. To aerate the water, he staked the pipe so that it tipped up at the outlet, splashing inflow on a rock set at the shoreline. (Usually it's well water that needs aeration; fish farmers are careful to check well water oxygen levels, splashing it over baffles or stones, if necessary.)

As always, the foremost cure for leaky ponds is to forestall it in the first place with proper siting. Use test pits and soil tests to check for clay. As Dubravius warned, "He that soweth in dust shall reap dust."

This past summer, late in August, four brook trout turned up dead in my pond. It wasn't a big fishkill, but it was a big disappointment. Those trout were the last of my biggest stocking—sixty fry put in two years before. It was 80 degrees F throughout the pond that weekend, hotter by ten degrees than the pond had ever been. The experts say that brook trout begin to die at 77 degrees F.

Later, I talked to an angler with thirty years of fishing Lake Champlain under his belt. He told me that it had been the hottest summer he'd experienced in Vermont. Worse, for the first time in memory, the walleyes wouldn't bite. Surface water had reached the high 60's, and the walleyes were lying low to avoid the heat. My friend is a snob about walleyes; he won't chase anything else; I'm crazy about brook trout. We lamented that if Vermont summers stayed so hot, our fishing habits would have to change.

I considered aerating the water and building a pier to cast extra shade, maybe even dumping in a load of ice cakes from an icehouse on the dam. But that seemed excessive against a more natural solution: rainbows. Rainbow trout are hardier than brookies; they can survive more stress, less oxygen, and temperatures up to 86 F. And if they don't taste like brookies, the difference is hardly worth the cost of a crop failure or mechanical surgery. Next summer, along with a gambler's crop of brookies, I'll be stocking rainbows.

Fall

Fall is busy on land, but on water, life quiets down. In fact, there's little to do, unless you count catching trout. When trout reach 10 to 12 inches it's time to make room for next year's crop. Otherwise you might see your big fish eat your stock. I never catch all the trout at once. Instead, the pond is a live cooler from September through November, and I harvest when the pan is hot. No fancy tackle involved, only an old spinning reel, a sharp hook with the barb filed off, worms or grasshoppers or bacon, and a bucket.

Laying down the pond for winter does mean keeping out leaves. Decaying leaves eat up oxygen under the ice and then come back to haunt you as slimy algae in summer. Here it's easy to rake submerged leaves from shore. In cool weather the water clears up, and sunken debris is in clear sight. There's not much: this is a self-cleaning pond. High up on a windy slope, the pond is swept by westerlies that shepherd leaves to the east bank where the spillway current draws them off. Only the leaves from some birches, maples, and one old apple tree are trapped against the spillway fish fence. It's simple to rake them away. On a breezy site the pond with downwind spillway grooms itself.

A final seasonal ritual comes with the first skating ice. My shadow glides beneath the transparent ice, skates carving powdery white calligraphy on the frozen pond. A brush pile stands on the dam, collected throughout the summer and fall. Twilight falls. I fire the brush. A deep orange reflection lights on the ice: the pond keeper's harvest moon.

Part III
In the Stream and Under Cover

The Digger: A Stream Pond that Carves Itself Under the Aquadome

The Digger: A Stream Pond that Carves Itself

One summer I swam in a stream pond in the second curve of an oxbow in Abbott Brook. The flow had chiseled into the bank, sweeping out a twenty-foot bowl, then doubled back where the roots of a poplar grove held the bank together. Rebounding sediment had settled into a sandy beach on the shallow bank. You could swim all day against the current and never get anywhere.

This stretch of brook with its whirly-pit was one of the brightest lures when the surrounding land was deeded to a young family from California. Lee Ann and Mike turned salvage from an old carriage house into a post-and-beam saltbox near the bank and counted on the pond for household water and summer baths. One summer afternoon, with some help from their daughter Heather, they laid up a stone dam to deepen the basin to six feet. They chopped down a poplar to bridge the brook—great for hanging by the knees in the free current. But with autumn rains came a tide of silt that filled the little pond, and ice and spring snowmelt crumpled the dam.

Just south, Dave and Victoria built a silo house out of dismantled Army barracks trucked from Michigan. It was a memorial to thrift and Sixties sentiment. Really monumental was their cellar sauna and front-yard pond. The sauna was about seven cubic feet. Clear cedar boards lined the interior and two racks of slatted benches criss-crossed the room. A mail-order sheet-metal stove burned with cheery red cheeks near a knee-high window that peered over a rocky brook. During tower construction David and Tor had let the brook run loose. With the house together, they looked around and decided to make a pond. They build a stone dam and shoveled silt out of the basin. The dam was laid up loose enough to pass the flow and contain a pool. It filled deep enough to inspire David, after a midnight sauna, to climb the ladder to his tower roof and leap for the dark pond below. But spring came with runoff that punched out the dam and swept in a load of silt—a nuisance for the rest of us and potentially fatal for David.

So a ritual grew in the summer. Neighbors gathered at different stream ponds for dam repair and silt shoveling. Given a good blend of hot sun and cold beer it was okay, until you got your toe crunched. I began to ponder a better solution. I found it in a fifteen-year old illustrated bulletin published by the New York State Conservation Department. "The stream pond," I read, "must lie *below* the dam." It's simple geology: pools form naturally in the wake of a waterfall.

"Log pyramid pool digger" is the title the conservationists tagged their pond making method, and it wasn't long before I saw how smoothly it worked. With my neighbors, Blake and Aletta, who live on the brink of Podunk Brook, I raised a barrier of logs and stones across the water, triggering a waterfall that carved out a pond. Now it flows like a self-propelled excavator and even sweeps itself clean every spring—a sorcerer's impoundment. We just call it the *digger pond*.

A sidehill pond is a bath; the digger is a whirlpool. Stillwater ponds lie under ice half the year; the churning digger pond freezes for two or three of winter's coldest months, at most. The digger attracts native trout without trapping them, simultaneously stirring up a richly-aerated pond suitable for cage-culturing fish. And it makes a fine sauna site.

As with all forms of pond making, success depends on tapping natural advantages of terrain. A stream has a way of hinting at the best site for a digger pond: a hollow that could be enlarged, a slow shallow flow between stable banks, or a pool already forming under existing falls. Banks should be at least three or four feet high, and sites prone to flooding avoided.

The size of the digger basin will be limited by the breadth of the stream, so look for a site wide enough to let you stretch out—"Ample and large, that the arms spread abroad might not be hurt," as Cicero described the ideal pond—but not so wide that finding dam materials is difficult, or where watershed runoff will overload the structure. A stream spanning ten to twenty feet, catching runoff from less than ten square miles, works well. Dam materials should be close at hand. Our digger dam was built with trees felled at the site. Round timbers about a foot in diameter make the best structure, with hemlock, cedar, and tamarack topping the list. For longest durability the bark should be peeled. Stones can be used in place of timber, although the dam will be less effective, if quicker to build.

Dams are subject to a trio of wracking forces: sliding, crushing, and overthrow. A strong foundation will prevent sliding, and a tight structure will avert crushing and overthrow. The best foundation for a digger is bedrock or solid bottom. A base of sand or mud will undermine the structure. If you fail to find a solid base it may be possible to create one using an old loggers' technique for building stream-driven dams: drive a row of wooden pilings into the stream bed to keep the bottom from washing away and to form a base to which the sills of the dam can be bolted.

To be most effective, the dam should rest on a pair of sill timbers that traverse the stream, lying flat on the bottom and butted into the banks. To insure that the dam does not slide, an elaborate anchoring technique was suggested in the N.Y. State Bulletin. A trench is excavated about two feet wide, four feet deep into the banks, the base level with the stream bed. If stream water is high it may be diverted to one side by temporary dams made of logs or stone. Here on the Podunk, to save labor and comply with Vermont regulations against stream course alteration, we found low water construction best.

Drift bolts are used to pin the twin timbers to the stream bed, and an additional log is entrenched about four feet upstream. The sills are then tied to this anchor log with galvanized poultry wire. The pond maker drills one-inch holes every six feet or so in parallel sills and pins down the base by sledge hammering three-quarter inch concrete reinforcing bars through the logs, deep into the stream bed. Six-foot lengths of rebar sunk five feet deep leave a foot to crimp over and hold down the sills. Obstructions in the stream bed may be side-stepped by repositioning the bolts or backfilling and weighing down the butt ends of the sills. Additional drift bolts should be pinned two feet to either side of the joints. The six-inch anchor log is then entrenched about four feet upstream of the sills, flush with the stream bed, and drift-bolted or otherwise firmly secured. The chicken wire is then used to tie the sills to the anchor, as well as create a ramp to sweep water over the dam. The wire is blanketed over the width of the stream and secured to the anchor log and sills with galvanized nails or staples. Fine brush is layered over the wire and anchored with flat stones to complete the seal. Finally, two logs of similar girth are fitted into the sill crevice and spiked at the outside ends, leaving a mid-stream gap of a foot or two. The central opening is then cut wide enough to pass the entire flow of the stream into the center of the pond. This trimming should be synchronized with a run of low water. Additional spikes are added to secure the logs, with an eight-inch board nailed over the exposed sills to cleat the wire.

Of course, nothing in the world of natural stream ponds resembles such a structure. Aletta, Blake, and I didn't hesitate to assemble a simpler digger dam. We bridged the stream with a pair of balsam timbers, anchored the butts with stones, and backfilled the upstream side with more stones. By adding a rim of stones at the downstream end of the pond, Aletta made sure that even in a drought the pond spans fifteen feet with four or five feet of water.

Blake and Aletta are guaranteed a regular catch from the pond in season. And since the pond is cupped at the head of a stretch of water that flows dead south, it gathers direct and reflected sun. Last summer Blake built a sauna at the northwest end of the pond, taking advantage of the sun to supplement the sauna's wood fire. Through all but the deepest freezes the pond stays clear for sauna baths. If their household water freezes up, the digger pond holds a reservoir of emergency water.

"It looks like a backwards dammed pond," Blake said a while back, soaking under the falls between saunas. "But it sure does work."

Low-water summertime is the season for digger pond making. In the background at Aletta and Blake's, sauna makers are also at work.

Digger dams are often used to carve the trouble-free reservoirs for offset ponds. Here a small digger collects stream water to feed a nearby pond sited in dry terrain. Water cascading over the dam simultaneously fills the basin and sweeps sediment away from the feed pipe, which lies just beneath the surface, plugged into a cement block. The pipe runs 100 yards downhill to the offset embankment pond.

The digger dam is sloped and stepped to regulate streamflow through notches spanning the pool. Rot-resistant hemlock 2 × 2's sunk into the banks keep the flow from working around the flanks. Spanning the downstream end of the digger pool, a loose-stone dam helps contain water. The pipe is 4" PVC.

One hundred yards downhill from the digger pond lies an offset embankment pond.

1) Dig two trenches across the stream bottom and four feet into the banks. Lay two logs in the downstream trench and one in the upstream, anchored with one-fourth inch reinforcing rods. Site the trenches roughly four feet apart.

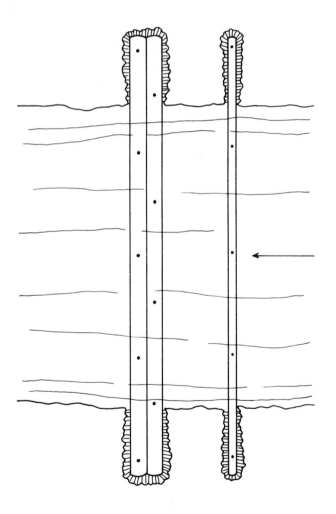

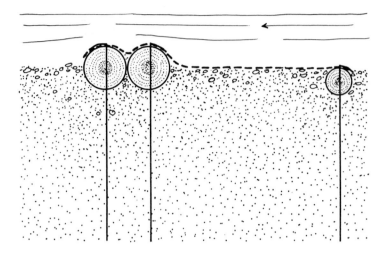

2) Lay two inch mesh wire over the logs and stream bottom, stapled to the logs.

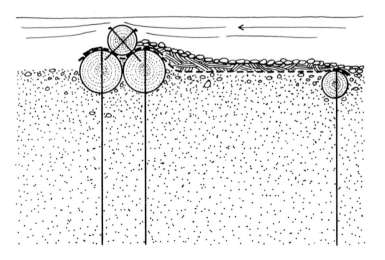

3) Spike smaller logs to the top of the downstream logs, leaving a midstream gap of one or two feet. Fasten only the outer ends of the top logs to the sills.

4) Cover the wire mesh with brush and then stones. Anchor the log ends with soil and rocks. Now the notch should be enlarged by cutting back on each log alternately from the center of the spillway until the entire flow of the stream passes through. This opening should be cut during an average low water period. Add spikes to secure the topside logs. Once the center opening is set, nail down an eight inch wide board to the two sill logs to cover the exposed wire.

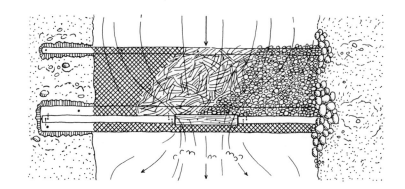

5) The digger dam carves, cleans, and aerates the in-stream swimming hole. It will flow ice-free two or three months longer than a still water pond.

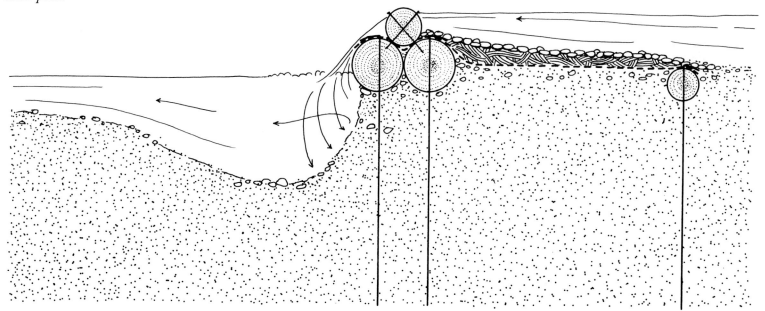

Under the Aquadome

Here is Eden in a thimble. Lush vegetation snakes around a steamy green lagoon, fish school beneath a splashing waterfall, and condensation drips languorously from overhead. An occasional insect buzzes through the tropical air. This aquadome is unheated, in the conventional sense, but its temperatures remain moderate year-round—despite winter temperatures that may scrape 30 degrees below zero Fahrenheit.

Viewed from the outside, this geodesic hump seems to fit the season: beehive in July, igloo in January; by night it glows like the rising moon. Year round, since 1974, Robert and Ellie Huke have tended this homemade nirvana-under-a-dome, annually raising three crops of vegetables and two harvests of fish. Daily, the Hukes cut herb garnishes and salad greens, pull onions, radishes or salsify, and cast a handful of feed into the small pond.

When their frost-wary neighbors are just planting the summer garden, the Hukes are already gathering cucumbers and tomatoes, enjoying a two-month jump on the short New England growing season. In the late fall they harvest more than 80 three-quarter-pound *tilapia*—a direct descendant of the "fishes and loaves" of parable fame—and stock the pond with 50 brook trout fingerlings. By May Day, they are ready to haul out 40 pounds of gourmet-quality trout and replace them with the warm water-loving tilapia for another summer. Lettuce, peas, collards, cabbage, tomatoes, beet greens, spinach and cucumbers thrive in the pond-side garden.

The Huke aquadome looks to me like the most success-ful approach to bringing a pond under cover. Other methods of indoor aquaculture range from raising fish in recycled oil barrels under lights in the basement to using fish tanks or translucent fiberglass tubes that double as heat sinks in solar greenhouses. However, unlike indoor ponds that require integration into solar-oriented, super-insulated houses (or basements), the Huke aquadome stands as an independent system that essentially takes care of itself. Like an earth pond, it sits comfortably away from the house, blending equally well with an underground home or 18th century farmhouse. Adding one to a homestead involves no expensive retrofitting.

The story of the evolution of the Huke aquadome is a primer on the art of indoor pond culture. The aquadome evolved out of Robert Huke's research into global agriculture and geography—he is a professor of geography at Dartmouth College—and a killer frost that descended on his garden tomatoes.

"Our original idea was to gain a longer growing season," Huke recalls. "We began planning to trap solar energy in a greenhouse structure, but I wanted to avoid the usual wild range of temperatures in a greenhouse—too hot in the day, too cold at night, like a car with its windows raised. We had to have a heat sink, something in which we could store heat during the hottest part of the day and which would readily release it at night. Water turned out to be the best heat sink we could think of."

Professor Huke introduces the spring stocking of young tilapia to the aquadome pool.

Heat sink is a term that brings to mind expensive solar components, but what Huke turned to was the bottom section of a pre-formed concrete septic tank, capable of holding 1500 gallons of water. The water in the tank could absorb the excess heat of the day in the greenhouse and, in the cool of the night, yield up this warmth to stabilize growing temperatures. The tank would remain uncovered, allowing water to evaporate from the surface of the pond. Rather than being lost, however, it would condense on the skin of the greenhouse and drip back down, enhancing foliar irrigation of vegetable crops and creating the sort of warm, humid atmosphere in which most plants revel.

By miniaturizing the earth's hydrologic cycle in a closed structure, Huke believed that he could eliminate the problems that plague farmers and gardeners everywhere. Drought would never be a concern, nor flood; water would be recycled constantly with a minimum of loss (Huke cites the example of a commercial 3840-square-foot greenhouse in southern California that produces tomatoes and uses less water in a day than a typical five-person household in the same area). Frosts and sudden shifts of temperature would be eliminated. The threat posed by rabbits, groundhogs, deer, and other predators could be forgotten, and insect intrusions easily controlled.

Huke might have liked to bring an entire pond and garden indoors, but the original fantasy of a huge dome was limited by reality—the "oil shock" of 1973. Huke had decided to cover his structure with PVC plastic; but, with motorists lined up at the gas pumps and supplies of many petroleum-based materials threatened, the best and widest plastic he could find was 10-mil material in 54-inch-wide rolls. Accordingly, he decided to build a dome with a maximum span in each triangle of 52 inches, allowing two inches for secure stapling.

The decision to use a geodesic dome was made to admit the maximum amount of light at all times of year and to conserve materials. Huke says that in greenhouses less than 30 feet across, geodesic shapes are the least expensive per covered square foot, with the smallest volume of air to ground area covered—making it easier to heat and cool. He says geodesic structures have great strength, are able to withstand strong winds and snow loads, but are built with small, easy to handle components.

Having access to a computer, with the aid of colleague Robert Sherwin, Huke determined that—with the available plastic film—they could build a dome 17.1 feet in diameter, with an eight-foot peak. The skeleton of the dome was built of high-stress, clear, southern pine, with no knots or weak points.

Huke started with 18 pieces of ten-foot lumber, ripping them in half to create strut material that measures one and five-eighths inches square. (Other dome builders might find it easier to start with two-by-two-inch lumber and avoid ripping.) The computer print-out indicated that the two strut sizes needed were 56.3 inches and 63.6 inches, which meant that each ten-foot length of wood could yield one of each without waste. Twenty-three circular hubs cut from aluminum and a bucket of rustproof, cadium-plated, two-and-one-quarter-inch bolts were used to cinch the frame together.

Close to their house the Hukes had found a level, sunny, well-drained site for the dome. A slope of tall pines buffered the north wind. The setting seemed ideal. A backhoe operator was hired to dig a four-foot-deep hole, carved in the circumference of the dome shape. Ten five-foot-long cedar posts were next installed at intervals around the periphery of the excavation, driven one foot into the ground at the bottom of the hole, and used to support the base hubs of the dome.

From ground level down, the Hukes inserted two-inch foam insulation to help conserve the heat of the dome's soil. They levelled the pit bottom and covered it with three inches of sand. A truck rigged with a crane delivered the concrete septic tank, setting it in the center of the pit, with its long axis running north-south.

Next, the Hukes dug a ditch from the house to the dome, installed an underground electric cable, and filled both the trench and the dome pit with soil.

Because of its portability, the dome skeleton was built near the site and then moved onto its permanent foundation. A few friends appeared to help carry the dome frame to its cedar post foundation, where it was anchored with bolts and wire and treated with wood preservative.

The nine most northerly panels were covered with one-and-a-half-inch foam, its foil facing inside, to insulate against north winds and to reflect back the light coming in from the south. To carry the expected weight of snow on top of the dome, the five panels at the peak were covered with premium-grade fiberglass. The balance of the dome was then skinned over with ten-mil polyvinyl plastic, stapled to the outside of the struts.

The basic structure of the aquadome was now complete. The Hukes filled the 34-inch-deep pond; and the water warmed quickly, moderating temperature extremes as they had predicted. They had created a longer growing season within the greenhouse, and additional possibilities quickly presented themselves.

"It seemed a waste to have all that water inside the dome, and not be able to use it in some way," says Huke.

"So we decided to put fish in."

The Hukes were already well-informed about aquaculture and about wild fish as well. Together they have researched fish farms in Burma, the Philippines, and the United States; and they keep their cellar stocked with angling gear and their freezer packed with bass and walleye caught from local waters. They knew that the first requirement of good fish production was good water. Rejecting the chlorinated town water, they hung gutters along the eaves of their house to catch rainwater for the aquadome pond.

To bring the system to life, the Hukes installed a water circulator. This pump and filter assembly is the heart of the aquadome. Without it, waste would quickly accumulate and poison the fish. They linked two 55-gallon oil drums together with a two-and-a-half-inch pipe, four inches from the bottom. The tops were removed, the drums thoroughly cleaned, and the exteriors painted black to absorb heat. A couple of heavy-duty beams were bridged across the width of the dome pond at its south end, and the barrels placed on top. Both barrels were packed with Actifil (multi-faceted black plastic matrices, each the size of a spool of thread). A submerged pump capable of circulating 600 gallons an hour was installed to take water from the bottom of the pond, run it through the barrels of Actifil and return it over a four-foot waterfall.

The purpose of this arrangement was to recycle the fish slough through the barrels, where the matrices would host a fuzz of algae. Thriving on the nitrogen in the fish waste, the nitrifying bacterial bloom would convert ammonia in the water to nitrite. The water would then splash into the pond, replenishing oxygen, and enabling the nitrite to become nitrate, which is harmless to fish. In

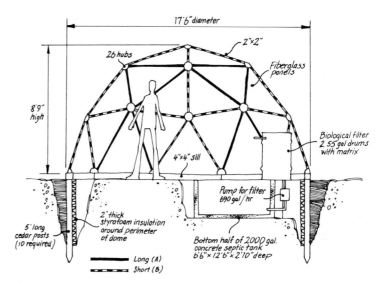

Cross-sectional diagram of the 17.5 foot Huke aquadome. Diagram by Ian Grainge.

addition, the streaming waterfall would enhance the humidification of the aquadome.

Huke's sleight of hand worked: he condensed the planet's hydrologic cycle. What the earth did naturally, he duplicated in a dome with a water circulator and half a septic tank. Material costs in 1974 were roughly $1000.

Next came the stock. "We knew we would need two kinds of fish," says Huke. "The water gets very warm in summer and quite cold in winter, although no ice has formed in five years. So we wanted one kind of fish that would do well in warm water and one kind that would do well in cold water. We chose catfish for the summer crop and brook trout for the winter." While it is true that rainbow trout can withstand greater stress and higher temperatures than brook trout, the Hukes knew that rainbows don't taste as good until they exceed 12 inches. Hence the brookie was choosen for the five-month winter season in the aquadome.

That first fall the Hukes stocked the dome pond with 50 four-inch brook trout fingerlings. Throughout the winter the fish grew on a daily ration of commercial trout chow in water that never fell below 37 degrees Fahrenheit, although temperatures outdoors dropped as low as 20 below zero.

But trouble began when the frisky trout began banking their turns against the abrasive concrete tank, scraping off their protective mucous layer. "They started going crazy," says Huke. He solved the problem by draping rolled plastic down the pond walls. To supplement their feed, he experimented with a wire mesh rack of rotting garbage suspended over the pond. "I was hoping to grow flies for the fish, but the dome got too hot for the flies and they died. So I stayed with the trout chow."

Last December, while the trout were still small and their oxygen requirements were low, Huke turned off the water circulator. For a month he left it off, and the fish were untroubled. "People had been asking me how much it cost to operate the pump," says Huke, "so I talked to some engineering students, and they figured it came to about three cents a day. But when I looked at the bill for a month I couldn't see any difference at all! The cost must be very small."

Soon after Huke put the pump back into operation, he was startled by a fishkill in the aquadome. "One morning I walked out to feed the fish and there were dead trout all around the pond! Ten of the fish had leaped out. So I raised the freeboard around the tank with 10-inch planks and that stopped it. A while later I figured it out—the trout were responding to the waterfall pouring out of the barrels. They were trying to jump up the cascade and swim upstream."

All winter, vegetables around the pond grew in soil of composted sludge supplemented with waterings of fish slurry. Phosphate was spaded into the soil to balance the nitrogen-heavy irrigation, which tended to produce leggy plants.

By mid-April, with pond-side peas knee-high and cucumber plants scaling a trellis to the top of the dome, the trout measured about 12 inches each. When the fish began to act logy, a sign of warmwater stress in the 70 degree F water, the Hukes set about harvesting. They used small poles, four-pound monofilament lines, and barbless hooks baited with garden worms. The trout averaged three-quarters of a pound, having more than doubled in length during five of the coldest months of the year.

The Hukes at first encountered unexpected difficulties

in cultivating vegetables under the dome. Young Brussels sprouts set out in the greenhouse in December grew, surviving the cold of January but bolting to flower as soon as warmer weather arrived in late March. The Hukes had discovered the biennial nature of Brussels sprouts, which normally produce a head the first year and a flower stalk and seeds the second. In the below 50-degree *F* temperatures of mid-winter, the plants had been stimulated to enter directly into their reproductive phase. By moving the planting date up to March first, these problems were eliminated.

The heat of summer also brought its share of surprises. The New Alchemists had conducted similar experiments with covered ponds; but the Hukes were breaking relatively new ground for themselves, and they made a number of classic mistakes. Believing that they could keep out insect pests and create very high humidity and temperatures in the summer months, they kept the dome tightly shut and waited for their plants and fish to flourish. Recording their experiences in a book, *A Fish and Vegetable Grower For All Seasons,* Huke wrote:

> "Keeping the dome tightly closed did have one positive effect. Never did we lose so much as a single leaf to an insect pest—the bugs just couldn't survive the heat. For the plants, however, it was a different story. By mid-July we had a riot of vegetative growth, so much that it became difficult to move inside. Tomato plants were six feet tall, two climbing spinach plants had already reached the peak of the dome eight feet above the water, and the muskmelon vine had climbed to the peak, fallen back to the soil, crept across the fish tank via a 2-by-12-inch plank and was climbing up the far side of the dome. In one 24-hour period it grew 12½ inches. At the end of July the vine was covered with blossoms and we could hardly wait for the bushels of giant muskmelons to be harvested from this single plant. It continued to grow and we continued to wait.

> "In imitation of the bees that were not to be found in the dome, we fertilized the blossoms manually with a tiny brush, but gradually the blossoms withered and fell. Eventually the plant reached a total length of 42 feet, never setting a single fruit. Perhaps the reason for our lack of fruit that first summer is told by the following story.

> "On August 12 at 4:30 in the afternoon we opened the door of the dome and entered. Immediately we were stopped by an invisible wall. Within seconds our skin felt as if thousands of needles were piercing us. We couldn't breathe and perspiration exuded from every pore. A quick look at the recording instruments told graphically of our problem. The water temperature was 96 degrees Fahrenheit, the relative humidity was 100 per cent and the air temperature was 135 degrees Fahrenheit. A human could live in that environment for a short time only and most insects for a time shorter still. Even the catfish were at the upper level of tolerance and the plants had been pushed too hard. There was unbelievable vegetative growth but no fruiting whatever. Sweet potato plants over six feet tall produced miniscule tubers, and the other plants nothing. Only after the weather cooled considerably did the

eggplants finally produce a bountiful yield. We knew that for success in succeeding summers the plants could not be subjected to such extreme conditions."

To vent off the heat and summer steam, Huke hinged a panel at the top so that it could be opened and closed and installed a solar fan powered by photovoltaic cell to stir a breeze whenever the sun shone. The door to the dome is now left open in hot weather.

A crop of 100 four-inch channel catfish fingerlings had been stocked in the pond following the trout harvest, and these reached a length of 12 inches by November 15, despite the fact that they had disappeared in the pea-soup-colored pond water for their entire growing season. This algal bloom, a natural occurrence in the warm weather, helped feed the catfish, who also consumed 50 pounds of trout pellets over the summer. Augmented with scraps from the cleaning of game fish, the diet turned four pounds of fingerlings into 52 pounds of harvested catfish. Some of these went directly into the freezer, while others were hickory-smoked before freezing.

Although pleased with the performance and taste of the catfish, the Hukes now stock the summer pond with tilapia, a peaceful fish of African origin that grazes on algae and shows a better growth rate and feed-consumption ratio than catfish. Tilapia are noted for the ease with which they can be bred in captivity and for their unusual breeding habits; after eggs are spawned and fertilized, the female tilapia gathers them in her mouth to hatch. The fry spend their first days in this protective environment, during which time the mother stops eating altogether. Gradually the tiny tilapia begin to venture forth, returning to the female's mouth for safety until they no longer fit or are turned away.

Tilapia also reach sexual maturity at an early age, which can be a drawback in intensive pond culture. Rather than growing, they can expend great amounts of energy in courtship, and it is now considered preferable to raise the sexes separately. The Hukes buy 80 to 90 male tilapia measuring about two inches each from Mike Sipes, a breeder in Palmetto, Florida, and in the seven months between April and November they normally reach a length of nine inches. While only 70 percent of the catfish survived, not one tilapia was lost in the first summer that Huke tried them. "We stocked 87 two-inch fingerlings and harvested 87 nine-inchers about 12 ounces each. It's crazy but true!" The pond is regularly doused with composted sheep manure to sustain the bloom of algae upon which the tilapia graze. Because replacement rainwater for the pond lacks nitrogen and phosphate, a supplement of bone meal is added periodically. Pond water is monitored to maintain a pH of about 6.5. The circulation system maintains water oxygen levels between five and six parts per million.

When water temperatures cool down to about 58 degrees F, usually in late November, the Hukes drain the pond and prepare the tilapia for the freezer. The septic tank is scrubbed down, rinsed out, and refilled with rainwater. The filter is thoroughly cleaned, yielding several pounds of rich fish wastes for their outdoor garden. The barrels are scoured and rinsed with rainwater before the filter system is replaced. The pond is now ready for stocking with 40 or 50 four-inch brook trout.

"Our last crop of tilapia was beautiful," says Huke. "It took me about a day to clean them up and wash out the tank, and they sure did smell. But Ellie cooked up a batch with sweet-and-sour sauce, and our daughter Debbie took the first bite. 'Hey, not bad,' she said. Not bad!

Well, they were excellent!''

Since that first year the Hukes have made a few changes in the aquadome. The fragile PVC dome skin peeled away in a strong wind during the first winter, and they replaced it with lightweight Kalwall SunLite fiberglass, a rigid greenhouse material with excellent light-transmission characteristics. This raised the cost of the dome $160 by the time Huke had purchased the fiberglass, bolts, and nails—a cost that would be a necessity for a durable structure.

One strut started to rot, and Huke found that it was easy to remove and replace, which allayed his fear that a breakdown of any one strut might cause the collapse of the whole structure. No further rotting has occurred, although Huke scrapes some moss from the struts that receive the most moisture.

While the Huke aquadome will surely undergo further refinements, it has been successful enough to convince its builder that large-scale aquadomes may represent a serious alternative for food production in the future. Huke doesn't see aquadomes blanketing North American wheat fields, nor as a substitute for all open-field agriculture. Rather, he envisions the use of commercial-scale units to supply small communities or even co-operative groups with fresh vegetables throughout the year.

Even without additional heat, he says, the growing season in New England would be increased to 270 days. Supplemented with warmth from solar systems and aided by energy from wind or solar generators, aquadomes could become year-round greenhouse-fish farms.

For the time being, however, the 17-foot dome in the Huke backyard continues to supply both food and something equally important:

"After a long and busy day at the office with the phone ringing constantly," says Huke, "what could be more relaxing than a few minutes in the dome — no phone, no radio, the damp earth smelling of growing plants and the water cascading from the filter as a miniature waterfall. As one enters the dome, the trout start jumping for their evening ration. Inside the dome one is in a world apart, separated for awhile from the pressures of 20th century society and surrounded by a mini-world of one's own creation."

Appendix
Pond Culture Resources

Please consult Books in Print, your local Cooperative Extension Service, the Soil Conservation Service, or the US Government Printing Office for current availability of books, pamphlets and brochures.

BOOKS

Axelrod, Herbert. *Koi of the World: Japanese Colored Carp*. T.F.H. Publications, 211 West Sylvia Avenue, P.O. Box 27, Neptune City, NJ 07753

Bardach, John E. *Aquaculture: The Farming and Husbandry of Freshwater & Marine Organisms*. John Wiley & Sons, Inc., 605 Third Avenue, New York, NY 10016

Bennett, George W. *Management of Lakes and Ponds*. Van Nostrand Reinhold Company, 135 West 50th Street, New York, NY 10020

Brown, E. Evan. *World Fish Farming: Cultivation and Economics*. Avi Publishing Company, Westport, CT 06880

Curtis, Brian. *The Life Story of the Fish*. Dover Publications, Inc., 11 East Second Street, Mineola, NY 11501

Edwards, David J. *Salmon and Trout Farming in Norway*. Fishing News Books LTD, One Long Garden Walk, Farnham, Surrey, England

Kabish, Klaus and Joachim Hammerling. *Ponds and Pools—Oases in the Landscape*. Arco Publishing, Inc., 215 Park Avenue, South, New York, NY 10003

Limburg, Peter. *Farming the Waters*. Beaufort Books, 9 East 40th Street, New York, NY 10016

Reid, George K. *Pond Life*. Golden Guide Series, Western Publishing Company, Inc., 1220 Mound Avenue, Racine, WI 53404

Russell, Franklin. *Watchers at the Pond*. Time Reading Program, Time, Inc., Rockefeller Center, New York, NY 10020

Sedgwick, S. Dummond. *Trout Farming Handbook*. Scholium International, Inc., 130-30 31st Avenue, Flushing, NY 11354

Walton, Isaak. *The Compleat Angler*. E.P. Dutton, 2 Park Avenue, New York, NY 10016

US Department of Agriculture Soil Conservation Service. *Ponds—Planning, Design, Construction*. Handbook Number 590, US Government Printing Office, Washington, DC 20402

PAMPHLETS

Aquaculture Development Program of the Department of Land & Natural Resources. *Aquaculture in Hawaii Newsletter*. Room 359, 355 Merchant Street, Honolulu, HI 96813

Garden Way Publishing. *Building a Pond for Food and Fun*. Garden Way Bulletin A-19. Garden Way Publishing, Schoolhouse Road, Pownal, VT 05261

Lilypons. *Lilypons Annual Water Gardens Catalog*. Lilypons, MD 21717 or Brookshire, TX 77423

Van Ness Water Gardens. *Water Visions: The Complete Guide to Water Gardening Annual Catalog*. 2460 North Euclid Avenue, Upland, CA 91786-1199

Submatic Irrigation Systems, *Submatic Drip Irrigation Catalog*. P.O. Box 246, Lubbock, TX 79408

Vermont Cooperative Extension Service. *Fish Farming in Vermont*. University of Vermont, 601 Main Street, Burlington, VT 05401

MAGAZINES

Aquaculture Magazine. (Bimonthly with Annual Buyer's Guide). Box 2329, Asheville, NC 28802

Canadian Aquaculture. (Five issues per year with Annual Buyer's Guide). 4611 William Head Road, Victoria, BC V8X 3W9

Farm Pond Harvest Magazine. (Four issues per year). R.R. 3, Box 197, Momence, IL 60954

MAPS

Raised Relief Topographic Maps
TSI Supply, P.O. Box 151, Flanders, NJ 07836
Write for index map

United States Geographical Survey Maps,
Map Distribution Branch
Box 25286, Denver Federal Center, Denver, CO 80225

ORGANIZATIONS

California Aquaculture Association
P.O. Box 1004, Niland, CA 92257
Newsletter, *California Aquatic Farming*

The New Alchemy Institute
237 Hatchville Road, East Falmouth, MA 02536
Newsletters, books, and workshops on small—scale aquaculture and farming.

US Trout Farmer's Association
P.O. Box 220, Harper's Ferry, WV 25425
Magazine, *Salmonid*, on the trout industry.

EQUIPMENT

Fishing Supplies and Pond Management

Aquaculture Research Environmental Associates
P.O. Box 1303, Homestead, FL 33090
305-248-4205

Aquatic Control, Inc.
P.O. Box 100, Seymour, IN 47274
812-497-2410

DM&J Aquatic Weed Control
Box 294, Hebron, IL 60034
815-648-4083

Memphis Net & Twine
2481 Matthews Avenue
P.O. Box 8331, Memphis, TN 38108
901-458-2656 / 1-800-238-6380

Nichols Net & Twine
RT 3, Bend Road, East St. Louis, IL 62201
618-876-7700

Staff Industires, Inc. (pond liners)
240 Chene Street, Detroit, MI 48207
1-800-526-1368

Water Test Kits—Ammonia, Carbon Dioxide, Dissolved Oxygen, pH, and Water Hardness

Hatch Chemical Company
P.O. Box 907
Ames, Iowa 50010
515-232-2533

Water Circulators and Aerators

Barebo, Inc.
Otterbine Aerators
P.O. Box 217, RD 2, Emmaus, PA 18049
215-965-6018

Enertech Corporation
Sparco Wind—Powered Water Pump
P.O. Box 420, Norwich, VT 05055
802-649-1145

Fresh Flo Corporation
Fresh Flo Aerators
RT 1, Highway 28, SW, Cascade, WI 53011
414-528-8236

Lake Aid Systems
Wind—Powered Water Circulator
Box 1262, Bismarck, ND 58501
701-222-8331

Wadler Manufacturing
Pondmaster Wind—Powered Aerator
RT 2, Box 117, Galena, KS
316-783-1355

FISH

Trout

Brown's Trout Hatchery
RT 362, Bliss, NY 14024
716-322-7322

Cedar Springs Trout Hatchery
RT 2, Mill Hall, PA
717-726-3737

Fernwood Limne, Inc.
Fish and Consulting Services
77 RT 9, Gansevoort, NY 12831
518-793-1282

Great Brook Trout Farm
RD 1, Plainfield, VT 05667
802-454-7721

Hy-On-A Hill Trout Hatchery
Box 308, Plainfield, NH 03781
603-675-6267

Imlay City Fish Farm
1442 N. Summers Road, Imlay City, MI 48444
313-724-2185

Jan L. Michalek
11830 Camp Ohio Road, NE, St. Louisville, OH 43071
614-745-2187

Mt. Lassen Trout Farm
Route 5, Box 36, Red Bluff, CA 96080
916-597-2222

Waterland
Route 242, Mountain Road
Montgomery Center, VT 05471
802-326-4215

Warm Water Fish—Bass, Bluegills, Common Carp, Channel Catfish, Hybrid Sunfish

John B. Fitzpatrick Fishery Management Service
214 East North Street, Dwight, IL 60420
815-584-2545

Opel's Fish Hatchery
RR 1, Box 51, Worden, IL 62097
618-459-3287

Triploid Grass Carp, White Amur, Bighead

Malone's Fish Farm
Highway 31 South, P.O. Box 158, Lonoke, AR 72086
501-676-2800